THE ULTIMATE GAME

Life Lessons From Sports

DAVID ROBINSON

Pacific Press®
Publishing Association
Nampa, Idaho | www.pacificpress.com

Cover design by Steve Lanto
Cover design resources from iStockphoto.com.
Inside design by Aaron Troia

You can obtain additional copies of this book by calling toll-free 1-800-765-6955 or by visiting http://www.adventistbookcenter.com.

Library of Congress Cataloging-in-Publication Data

Names: Robinson, David, 1986- author.
Title: The ultimate game / David Robinson.
Description: Nampa, Idaho : Pacific Press Publishing Association, [2019] | Audience: Grades: 4-6.
Identifiers: LCCN 2019002143 | ISBN 9780816365081 (pbk. : alk. paper)
Subjects: LCSH: Sportsmanship—Juvenile literature. | Athletes—Conduct of life—Juvenile literature. | Sports—Religious aspects—Juvenile literature.
Classification: LCC GV706.3 .R62 2019 | DDC 175—dc23 LC record available at https://lccn.loc.gov/2019002143

March 2019

Dedication

To God and all the people this book will reach.

Contents

Acknowledgments

There are key people in everyone's life that can help guide them down the right path. For me, those people have been my mom, who sacrificed for my benefit; my best man and brother Irving, we share an unbreakable bond; my groomsmen, who continually help mold me (Bobak, Michael, Ron, Steven, and Duncan); my close circle of friends who constantly help shape my perspective; my teachers who helped guide my writing career; Randy Fishell and the *Guide* team, who started me off on a good foundation with The Sports Zone; *all* the athletes I coached/mentored along the way that helped contribute to my stories; and last but not least, my loving wife, Sasha, and our soon-to-be-born daughter, Sydney. Thank you all for your encouragement and support. May the words found in this book help bring spiritual clarity for what you believe in.

For more sports stories with spiritual perspective, check out sportszonestories.com.

Preface

"OK, Randy, I'm going to hand off the football to you on the next play." I could hardly believe my ears. Had the quarterback lost his mind? Sure, I was a member of the school intramural football team, but I was a second-string halfback—and the slowest player on the entire team! Then I realized the quarterback's ploy: our opponents would be caught off guard. It was a brilliant call, and I scored a touchdown.

I don't know if I ever told David Robinson that story. I might have, because I had the pleasure of working with him during the time he was a journalism intern at *Guide*. At six feet four, he cast a long shadow over my office desk.

David knows sports, both as a player and coach. But to him, any sports field is also a field for sharing the love of God. A stadium or an arena is a place for him to coach kids and others in critical spiritual and life skills.

In sports, David's abilities sets him apart from the wannabes. As a writer, he has an uncommon gift for drawing life-changing lessons from stories of remarkable athletes, memorable games, iconic coaches, and more. Most important, when it comes to pointing readers to Jesus, David consistently scores in the triple digits.

If your life revolves around celebrating base hits and hat tricks, you're going to love this book. And even if you aren't athletic and don't have any interest in who is likely to win the Super Bowl this year, you'll still find yourself sticking with these inspiring stories. After all, who doesn't want to be a winner?

—Randy Fishell
editor, *Guide* magazine, 1999–2016

Soccer

Tripped Up by Cheating

On June 22, 1986, one of the most infamous goals in *Fédération Internationale de Football Association* (FIFA) history took place. It occurred in the second half of a soccer match between Argentina and England.

Argentina's star player, Diego Maradona, slipped behind England's flank and received a wonderful lob pass. England's goalkeeper came out to swat the ball away as Maradona jumped up to head it. But instead of a header, Maradona faked it and intentionally used his hand to throw the ball into the net.

Unfortunately, the ref didn't have a good angle on the play and missed the dirty deed. Argentina went on to win the game. Afterward Maradona told reporters about the goal: "*Un poco con la cabeza de Maradona y otro poco con la mano de Dios*" (a little with the head of Maradona and a little with the hand of God).* Argentina

* Matt Bonesteel, "Diego Maradona Admits Video Replay Would Have Erased His 'Hand of God' Goal," *The Washington Post*, July 26, 2017, https://www.washingtonpost.com/news/early-lead/wp/2017/07/26/diego-maradona-admits-video-replay-would-have-erased-his-hand-of-god-goal/?noredirect=on&utm_term=.3a74034c9f78.

won the World Cup that year, and Maradona was named MVP of the game.

Maradona showed no remorse for his blatant cheating. In fact, he was more or less rewarded for it! But what exactly does it mean to cheat? Is it simply going against what's defined in the rule books? Is it cheating if you purposely step on another player's shoes during a game to trip them? What about intentionally hitting a player on the opposing team when no one is looking? Is it cheating only if a referee catches you?

Public shame and apologies are the future for anyone who gets caught bending the rules. However, what if you've perfected the art of cheating—you're so good at it that you have never gotten caught and never will? How does that fit in with your Christianity?

Now we're moving into the realm of pride. Pride will tell you that hard work isn't enough sometimes and that it's unacceptable for you to ever lose. Pride will tell you to cheat, deceive, and connive to win—but you shouldn't listen. After all, Satan's pride got him kicked out of heaven.

Basketball Hall of Famer Kareem Abdul-Jabbar observed: "In athletics there's always been a willingness to cheat if it looks like you're not cheating. I think that's just a quirk of human nature."*

Abdul-Jabbar is right. We can't help the fact that we were born into sin, but we can fight it. Listening to that still small voice (a.k.a. the Holy Spirit) will help us make the right decisions.

Proverbs 11:3 says: "Honesty guides good people; dishonesty destroys treacherous people" (NLT). So the next time you're tempted to cheat, remember that pride goes before a fall. And to all those who think they're too good to lose: you're trippin'.

I would prefer even to fail with honor than to win by cheating.
—Sophocles

* "Kareem Abdul-Jabbar Talkasia Transcript" CNN.com, July 2, 2005, http://www.cnn.com/2005/WORLD/asiapcf/07/08/talkasia.jabbar.script/index.html.

Power Source

In 1966 the *FIFA* World Cup was stolen. As part of an exhibition for the public, the trophy was supposed to go on display so that everyone could see it up close. The trophy was supposed to be under guard at all times. Unfortunately, the day after it was shown to the public, the trophy went missing. One of the guards noticed that the display case had been forced open. It seemed as though the culprits had probably escaped through a back door, because the wooden bar that normally kept the door closed was lying on the floor. Just as in any great heist movie, the finest police in London were brought in to help solve the case. While the police were busy looking for the suspects, Joe Mears, the chairman of the English Football Association, received a ransom note from an anonymous source. The note stated that unless Mears paid £15,000 (about $42,000 in today's US currency), the trophy would be melted down into gold bricks. Mears was told not to contact anyone, but he ignored that and contacted Detective Inspector Buggy. Long story short, Detective Buggy caught a suspect by using fake ransom money. Later a dog named Pickles found the trophy.

When you look at the big picture, the plan started out OK, but went downhill quickly. Sadly, those weren't the first culprits to experience that kind of failure. In 1 Samuel 4–6, the Philistines managed to defeat the Israelites in battle. Adding insult to injury, the Philistines took the Israelites' most prized possession: the ark of the covenant. This was the special place where God dwelled and had spoken to Moses. It also carried some sacred items concerning God's history with His people. After they stole it, the Philistines had nothing but bad things happen to them while the ark was in their possession. In the cities that it went to, the citizens got tumors, and hordes of rats invaded them. Eventually the Philistines returned the ark to the Israelites, and the tumors and rats went away.

The unbelievable part to me is that in and of themselves, the trophy and the ark of the covenant didn't mean anything. They were just material things. Even if the trophy was never returned, it wouldn't mean that new champions couldn't be crowned. If it came down to it, a new trophy could be made. Same thing with the ark. Both the thieves and the Philistines thought that by stealing these items, they would have some sort of power. However, we know that our power doesn't come from material things. It comes from the One who made those material things—God. Our power doesn't come from crosses, idols, or anything else. It comes from God. Put your trust in Him, and you will never be let down or deceived.

God has a reason for allowing things to happen. We may never understand His wisdom, but we simply have to trust His will.
—Unknown, adapted from Psalm 37:5

Football

A Lesson in Humility

The day rookie Dez Bryant said no, his actions caused quite a stir in the Dallas Cowboys camp. On July 25, 2010, veteran Roy Williams asked Bryant to carry Williams's pads off the field. Bryant refused, stating that he "was here to play football, not carry someone else's pads." Williams thought Bryant was being disrespectful, but Bryant insisted that he wasn't. Eventually the two worked things out and moved on.

This takes me back to my rookie year on my basketball team. I was forced to carry the water bottles to and from games. If I ever forgot my "duty," my older teammates always reminded me. On one hand, I detested carrying water bottles because I felt it was beneath me. On the other hand, I knew that this was a way for me to earn respect from the older team members. It's sort of like doing chores; everyone in a family has to do them. So if my team was supposed to be "family," then this was something I needed to do.

Naaman had a similar experience. The great commander of 2 Kings 5 was a decent enough guy. He'd won many battles with the help of the Lord, but he had one major setback: leprosy. Thankfully, a servant girl told Naaman to find Elisha to be healed. When Naaman finally arrived at Elisha's door, he wasn't healed right away. There was no bright flash, no blaze of glory from heaven. Instead, Naaman was told to dip himself in the Jordan River seven times. No biggie, right? Wrong. The Jordan River was one of the dirtiest rivers in the land!

It angered Naaman that he was forced to dip in a dirty river, but then his servants counseled him: "My father, if the prophet had told you to do some great thing, would you not have done it? How much more, then, when he tells you, 'Wash and be cleansed'!" (2 Kings 5:13, NIV). After that, a humbled Naaman dipped himself into that dirty Jordan River seven times, and his skin was healed. (Side note: Jesus was baptized in the Jordan River.)

Unfortunately there are times when team initiation rituals can become harmful. That sort of hazing isn't constructive and shouldn't be tolerated. However, everyone can learn to be humbler. How and when you learn it is completely up to you, but the sooner the better!

If you have a degree of humility about you, you have the ability to take advice, to be coachable, teachable. A humble person never stops learning.
—Todd Blackledge

Zoom Through the Hole

In the National Football League (NFL), Emmitt Smith is considered the greatest rusher of all time. He made a living off of dashing in and out among would-be tacklers at breakneck speeds. While his highlight reel is exhilarating, the thought of his job is terrifying to me. Part of being a rusher is running through the holes in the defense. The rusher can't hesitate, because the hole is open for only a couple of seconds. Sometimes rushers have to run even before they can see the hole they are running toward. It's insane! They don't really have time to think about it—they just act. They're able to do this because they are so in tune with the game that they have a feel for where these holes are going to be. Watching this happen is breathtaking.

I was equally in awe when I first read about a young boy in the Bible by the name of David. In 1 Samuel 17, David walked up to the camp where Israel was fighting the Philistines. Now, most of the men were cowering in fear as Goliath (who was super tall, by the way) openly dissed God. When David heard this, he didn't think, he just acted. His immediate reaction was basically, "Why is this bum talking crazy about God?" To cut a long story short, David defeated Goliath with one small stone and a big piece of God's awesome power. That's all good for a happy ending's sake, but how do you think David was able to react so quickly? Why didn't he cower in fear like the rest of the Israelite army?

I believe it was because he was so in tune with God that responding with courage came naturally to him. Every day David had time to talk with God, write psalms, and make music that proclaimed God's glory. When it came down to crunch time, it didn't matter that Goliath was humongous. Just as when he'd killed the lion and the bear, David knew that with God's help he would slay Goliath. There was no hesitation—he showed no fear.

I remember in the 1990s when a popular clothing company made a big splash. The company was called No Fear. Everyone and their mother had a No Fear sticker to wear. People liked to wear these stickers because they let everyone else know that they weren't scared of anything. Presently No Fear isn't as popular, but you can still apply the company's message to Christianity. There's nothing to fear when God is on your side. Speed toward the great opportunity ahead of you.

Courage is resistance to fear, mastery of fear—not absence of fear.
—Mark Twain

SMH Excessive Celebration

Imagine your favorite NFL player running in for a touchdown. As soon as he crosses the goal line, he spikes the ball in celebration. However, the party doesn't stop there. He then gathers the rest of his players, and they perform some well-rehearsed choreography. The players may act like bowling pins as the player who scored the touchdown takes an imaginary ball and bowls a strike on his teammates.

This may look cool and can even be fun to watch, but Roger Goodell, NFL commissioner, deems such shows unnecessary. In fact, he dislikes them so much that he has instituted a rule that penalizes players for showing off. The penalty is called "excessive celebration." It costs the team fifteen yards, and players can be fined. Most athletes don't care and celebrate excessively anyway. Sometimes a team loses the game because of that penalty.

I don't understand why athletes feel the need to celebrate excessively. If you score a touchdown, hand the ball to the ref and keep it moving. My bigger question is: Why does Roger Goodell believe that excessive celebrations are bad? His critics have come up with the snarky joke that the acronym NFL stands for No Fun League, but I think his reasons are biblical.

Remember King Hezekiah in Isaiah? In chapter 38, Hezekiah got sick and prayed to God that he would get better. God heard his prayers and granted him fifteen extra years. Touchdown! And how did Hezekiah choose to show his gratitude? By excessive celebration.

Travelers from Babylon had heard about Hezekiah's miraculous recovery and wanted to see him. Hezekiah graciously accepted them into his courts, and because he was wealthy, he showed them just how rich he was. The Bible says that Hezekiah opened up his storehouses and showed them all the silver, gold, spices, and treasures of his kingdom. The visitors left in good spirits—but that's when the prophet Isaiah showed up. Isaiah told the king that God was not pleased with him and that his descendants' future would not be pleasant.

Hezekiah moronically responded, "At least there will be peace in my time" (see Isaiah 39:8). Had Twitter been around back then, I think Isaiah might've tweeted, "SMH @Hezekiah." (SMH stands for "shaking my head," in case you're not up on the lingo.)

The purpose of a penalty for excessive celebration is to teach us how to humble ourselves. Remember to thank God for everything He has blessed you with, because pride always comes before a fall.

Sense shines with a double luster when it is set in humility.
An able and yet humble man is a jewel worth a kingdom.
—William Penn

"Black Monday"

The final week in every NFL regular season, week 17, is always looming in the minds of NFL coaches. Week 17 is so threatening because the Monday after the regular season ends, coaches of teams who didn't make the playoffs face the possibility of being fired. This day is often referred to as "Black Monday."

Eight coaches were fired following the 2012–2013 NFL season. Out of thirty-two teams, just twelve teams made the playoffs. Out of the twenty teams who didn't make it into the playoffs, eight fired their coaches. That's almost half! It's an incredibly high firing rate, and it's also a lot of pressure. Every season the coaches try their hardest to avoid being fired. These coaches realize that they have an entire season to prove their worth. If at the end of that season they don't live up to the hopes of their general managers, they often get fired.

"Halls of Fame"

Each sport sets up a hall of fame, a memorial that commemorates great players. The terms of getting into the hall of fame are similar. Usually a player has to be retired for a certain amount of time, have the right credentials, and, most important, has to be voted in by a board of constituents.

At the end of a player's career, they are judged to see whether they're worthy enough to be officially remembered in their sport. There are some players who wait their whole lives to get into a hall of fame, but they never make it because they didn't meet the criteria.

Christians also have a judgment day. In fact, according to Revelation 14:7, it's going on right now: "The hour of His judgment has come" (NASB). Unlike players and coaches, though, we aren't ultimately judged by human standards. God is considering all the facts. If you've accepted Jesus as your Savior and responded in joy to His leading, you're good to go! If not, well, it will be a very sad day—much worse than when a coach gets fired.

We should live our lives as though Christ were coming this afternoon.
—Jimmy Carter

God's Pocket

In football, after a quarterback snaps the ball into play, the offensive line tries to create a pocket. This pocket usually consists of big blockers who make a wall of protection around the quarterback. While in the pocket, the quarterback is protected and has time to make throws.

Many people consider football players to have one of the most stressful jobs in sports, mainly because huge players on defense try to tackle the quarterback. No matter what is happening around him, the quarterback must remain calm and trust that his offensive linemen will do their job long enough for him to make the best throw.

In 2014, the NFL witnessed several "hybrid" quarterbacks who made plays outside the pocket. Many fans quickly fell in love with Colin Kaepernick, Cam Newton, and Robert Griffin III because of their ability to break out of the pocket and run past defenders. Players such as these are considered special because of their athleticism, and by comparison they make other quarterbacks look like statues.

The downfall of these hybrid quarterbacks is that they often rely too much on their athleticism rather than allowing their offensive line to protect them. Sadly, as the NFL playoffs approached, the hybrid quarterbacks showed almost no growth in their position. They were often plagued with injuries because of the hard hits they took when they stepped outside the pocket.

On the flip side, such quarterbacks as Tom Brady, Aaron Rodgers, and Peyton Manning, who know how to feel their way around the pocket, succeed. Why? Because they understand that there is more protection in the pocket than outside it. In order to be an effective "brick wall," an excellent defensive lineman in the NFL will usually weigh more than three hundred pounds and measure more than six feet tall. The last thing a quarterback wants is to be tackled by one of these mammoth players. Even the most athletic quarterbacks are better off playing inside the pocket.

Think about it like this: every time you wake up, it's as if you're lining up on offense. The defense is the enemy, and nothing would give them more pleasure than to tackle you. As you snap the ball into play, your offensive line forms the pocket around you. Even though there is nothing but chaos surrounding you, you're not worried, because your offensive line is made up of God and His angels. The only time you get into real trouble is when you depend on your own abilities and run outside the pocket of God's protection. Always remember that God's pocket never fails. Make the right decisions by staying inside it!

How precious is Your lovingkindness, O God! Therefore the children of men put their trust under the shadow of Your wings.
—Psalm 36:7, NKJV

Find Your Foundation

As soon as the newspapers got pictures of the event, the pressure was on. It was the first round of the 2017 NFL playoffs. The New York Giants were going to face the Green Bay Packers at Lambeau Field. In the NFL playoffs, it's single elimination, so if you lose, your season is over. Normally the week before a playoff game is filled with studying and extra practice to make sure that players are ready for the big game. However, the Giants' head coach, Ben McAdoo, gave his players a twenty-four-hour break in the week leading up to the game. They could do whatever they wanted with that time. So several players, including Odell Beckham Jr. and Victor Cruz, went to party on a boat in Miami. To make matters worse, on the day of their game at Lambeau Field those same players came out to warm up in shorts and no shirts. The temperature at the time was in the low teens. When asked why they were practicing without shirts in the dead of winter, the players said that the cold didn't bother them. Not surprisingly, the Giants went on to lose that game badly: 38–13.

Many reporters and commentators blamed the loss on the fact that some players acted as though they weren't taking the game seriously enough. Instead of going to party on their day off, those players would have been wiser to spend the time practicing or even resting. Instead of warming up without shirts on, they could have bundled up and practiced as normal.

Some may call the loss a coincidence, but the wise know about the law of cause and effect. Human nature is really predictable. If you're goofing off before an important event, chances are you're not going to perform well. However, if you take it seriously, good things are bound to happen.

There's an awesome parable that describes this exact process. In Matthew 7:24–27, there are two builders: one wise and one foolish. The wise builder found a solid foundation to build his house on, while the foolish builder just built his house on top of sand. Everything was fine during the good weather, but once the rain and winds came, only the house that was built on the rock remained standing.

If you want to be successful, you have to mirror the patterns of behavior that lead to success. Ultimately you are responsible for building your own house of success. Every brick in your house is determined by the little things you do. If you choose to stay focused instead of being distracted, you're that much closer to being successful on your foundation.

There are no shortcuts to building a team each season.
You build the foundation brick by brick.
—Bill Belichick

Run Your Route

Knowing and running your routes in football is crucial. A team's receivers must run their routes precisely. That means that if the route is a buttonhook, don't run a slant. If a route requires you to make a straight run for twenty yards and then make a forty-five-degree angle, don't make a sixty-degree angle. Precision is key. Defenders on the other team aren't going to let those receivers get open easily. More often than not, they have to work extremely hard just to get open for a second or even a millisecond. Sometimes the defensive coverage is so tight that quarterbacks can't throw directly to their receivers, so they have to throw to an open spot on the receiver's route in hopes that they'll get open to catch it. That takes an enormous amount of trust. If the receiver doesn't run the route, it makes it much harder to complete the pass.

Completing a pass in the NFL is key because it leads to bigger things, such as extending a drive, scoring a touchdown, and even winning the game. This is something I wish Jonah would have understood. Before we can even get to verse 4 in Jonah 1, he's already running the wrong route. God gave him specific instructions to go to Nineveh. He wanted to throw Jonah a pass, but Jonah wasn't running the right route. Instead, Jonah went in the opposite direction, to Tarshish. By not running his route, Jonah ended up experiencing what some might call a whale of a tale. You can read more about it in the book of Jonah—it's only four chapters!

Without ruining the story too much, let me tell you that Jonah ends up running the right route and eventually reaching Nineveh. God wanted him there to witness to the citizens of Nineveh so that they could be saved. By not running his route, Jonah almost put all of that at risk.

Believe it or not, God has multiple routes for all of us to run. Each route represents a different journey that He wants to take us on. But if we're too scared to run the routes, then, like Jonah, we'll miss our opportunity to be used to our potential. Sometimes our fears will act as a smothering defense and try to stop us. But this just requires us to trust God even more and run our correct routes in order to be a better witness for Him. When we faithfully run our route, it will lead to bigger things in our future. God's plans for us are beyond our wildest imaginations; we just need to run our routes.

In times of difficulty those brave enough to
stay the course will be victors in the end.
—Bo Schembechler

The Thrill of Victory and the Agony of Defeat

The Carter Cowboys football team was once described as "the greatest high school football team ever assembled," but despite all their accomplishments, they're still haunted by one misdeed.

They were a high school football team from Dallas, Texas. In 1988, the team was filled with super talented players. These guys were winning every game and crushing all opponents. But players have to keep their grades up to be able to play. The controversy happened when, shortly before that season's playoffs, one of the students was accused of not keeping his grades up in an algebra class. When the teams who had been beaten by the Carter Cowboys realized that one of the players may have been ineligible to play the whole time, they wanted to kick the team out of the playoffs. But through it all, the Carter Cowboys fought hard to stay in.

Every week was a struggle. On one hand, the Carter Cowboys had to keep beating teams to stay in the playoffs. On the other hand, the coaches and parents fought legal battles to keep the team eligible for the playoffs. It was a grueling ordeal, but in the end, the Carter Cowboys ended up winning the state championship.

This is where the story should've ended. Unfortunately, for some players it was only the beginning. After winning the championship, six players decided, for whatever reason, to get involved with armed robbery. Crazy, right? From there, everything spiraled downward. Those players went to court, and five of them went to jail. Even worse, the whole team was labeled as crooks, and worst of all, the team and the community that surrounded it lost its reputation.

Actions always have consequences. It's a lesson that King David never forgot. Early in his life he fought and defeated the giant Goliath. He was praised as Israel's new champion. Eventually he rose to power and became Israel's king. Unfortunately he let his fame get the best of him. On the day he saw Bathsheba, he immediately wanted her for his wife even though she was already married. David did a wicked deed and had her husband killed in battle. He thought that he had gotten away with it until God sent the prophet Nathan to visit him. You can read more about it in 2 Samuel 12. That one sin cost David a child and marred his and his family's reputation for the rest of his life.

Accomplishments should be celebrated, but don't let your glory outshine the One who should always be glorified. Everyone makes mistakes, but thankfully God forgives us when we ask sincerely. We just need to stay humble and let God guide.

Never let success get to your head. Never let failure get to your heart.
–Anonymous

Play to Win

Statistics have become a huge part of professional sports. Coaches and scouts use stats to determine whether a player is good. What started in baseball as a new strategy from Billy Beane has exploded into a must-have for every other sports team. I love studying stats to determine how good a player is, but then I think of Brett Favre.

In 2016, Favre was inducted into the Pro Football Hall of Fame, and for good reason. Among a host of other accolades, he retired as a Super Bowl champion, had been selected eleven times for the Pro Bowl, and won the NFL Most Valuable Player award three consecutive times. But even with all those amazing stats, Favre still holds the record for most fumbles, most times sacked, and most passes intercepted in the NFL. So with those bad records attached to his name, how did a player such as Favre make it into the Hall of Fame? He sums it up perfectly in his induction speech:

"When I look back over my 20 years, I can honestly

> tell you . . . I hold no regrets. Did we win every game? No. Did I make every throw? No. Did I make mistakes? More than I care to count. But I can tell you this: There was never one time where I did not give it all I could.
>
> "I've said this to my daughters, and I'll say it to any young person out there who is playing sports: Don't ever look back and regret not doing your best. . . . There are no second chances. When you're 25 and you wish you would have done something in high school, it's too late. Don't cheat yourself. Don't cheat your teammates. Work as hard as you possibly can. Lay it all on the line, and whatever happens, happens. But you won't look back in regret."*

What Favre is trying to say is that if you focus too much on your stats, you'll miss the point of the game—to win! Our stats should be a reflection of how we played the game, not the other way around. We should never look at how a game is played and then figure out how to have the best stats. That would be foolish. In fact, people who focus too much on their stats are called stat stuffers, and it's generally frowned on.

In our journey as Christians, we can't focus too much on the statistics either. It's less about doing the right thing and more about why we're doing it. Jesus reinforces that in Luke 21:1–4. Even though the rich put many coins into the offering, the widow who gave two coins gave the most. Actions speak louder than words, but Jesus is more concerned with our hearts than our actions. Don't play for stats. Play to win.

The main thing is winning. Stats aren't that important. . . .
In the end things will work themselves out.
—John Harbaugh

---

* Brett Favre, "Brett Favre Enshrinement Speech," Pro Football Hall of Fame, August 6, 2016, https://www.profootballhof.com/players/brett-favre/enshrinement/.

Baseball

Bad Calls

"I just cost the kid a perfect game," lamented first-base umpire Jim Joyce.

Detroit Tigers pitcher Armando Galarraga had retired the previous twenty-six batters and was one out away from the elusive perfect game. However, perfection would stay perched on its pedestal as Galarraga—or, actually, the umpire—fell short. The runner who should've been called out at first was ruled safe by Joyce. Slightly dejected, Galarraga went to the mound one last time and struck out the final batter. His scorecard for the night would read 9 IP, 0 ER, and one hit. One hit away from perfection.

When asked how he felt about Joyce's mistake, Galarraga responded, "Nobody is perfect. What am I gonna do?"

One of the worst parts about any officiated game is getting a bad call. I remember dozens of traveling violations and phantom fouls called against me in basketball, but as Galarraga said, "What am I going to do?" Sure, I could sit there and complain, but what good would that do? The officials won't overturn their calls even if your argument is very convincing. Again, what can you do? Nothing.

That's right: absolutely nothing. Like the old folks used to say, "Don't cry over spilled milk," meaning once milk is spilled, you can't pour it back into its container, so there's no point in worrying about it. Just clean it up and move on.

In the Bible, there were many people who could've cried over spilled milk. Take Job, for instance. Talk about bad calls! He went from happy to devastated within a matter of hours. He lost his land, livestock, and children all in one day. And let's not even discuss those unsightly boils on his skin. Obviously Job wasn't happy with what was going on around him, but what could he do? It even got so bad that he questioned God about why all of this stuff was happening to him. I don't think Job was ready for God's response. To see the entire conversation, be sure to check out Job 38:1–42:6.

Sometimes in life, just as in games, things happen that are out of your control. Sure, you can cry, whine, and even try to fight it, but trust me, it's no use. Eventually you'll realize that the best thing is to acknowledge what happened and move on. I mean, come on, it's not like officials will never make a bad call again. So just keep moving ahead–in games and, more important, in life itself.

The job of arguing with the umpire belongs to the manager, because it won't hurt the team if he gets thrown out of the game.
–Earl Weaver

Look At the Big Picture

In 2001, Billy Beane, general manager of the Oakland A's, lost in the first round of the playoffs to the New York Yankees. Adding insult to injury, several of his best players left the team and later joined the Yankees. This forced Beane not only to replace his star players but to do it on a tight budget.

He realized hitting that curveball would be close to impossible, so he decided to institute something called sabermetrics, pioneered by Bill James years earlier. Simply put, sabermetrics ignored the players' physical gifts and looked strictly at the numbers they put up. Beane integrated this new system in Oakland.

Many people on the A's staff didn't like the new approach. They argued that baseball was based on skills and intangibles, not numbers alone. Much to their chagrin, Beane ignored them and kept the system. At first the A's were dreadful, and many people wondered if the new system was a bust. But eventually the A's won a remarkable twenty games in a row—a new American League record. However, despite all their regular-season success, they again lost in the first round of the postseason.

Later the Boston Red Sox told Beane that they were going to use sabermetrics because it had worked so well in Oakland. They offered him a general manager position and a huge sum of money. But Beane turned it down because he felt that he hadn't succeeded in Oakland. Why? Because Oakland still hadn't won the World Series.

Even though he helped popularize sabermetrics enough that every team in baseball uses it, Beane still feels that he isn't successful. However honorable his humility is, Beane doesn't see the big picture.

This reminds me of the Israelites complaining to God about wanting meat in the desert. At some point Moses must've thought, *Really, guys?* The Israelites had been rescued from slavery in Egypt; they had seen the Red Sea parted; and they were eating manna, food from heaven! But the Israelites weren't paying attention to all those things, because they were so focused on where they had been rather than what God was doing for them now. Like Billy Beane, they couldn't see the big picture.

Getting caught up with worldly things dulls our vision to what's really important. In situations like these, always seek the bigger picture. It'll help you deal with the disappointing moments in sports—and in life as well.

Life goes on with or without you. Don't waste time sulking in the dugout. Just enjoy what God is doing.

Success is to be measured not so much by the position that one has reached in life as by the obstacles which he has overcome.
—Booker T. Washington

A Day to Remember

On July 4, 1939, New York Yankees player Lou Gehrig told the world that he was dying. For the previous few games players and fans had noticed that Gehrig wasn't performing as well as he'd used to perform. That's when Gehrig went to the doctor to get himself checked out.

The doctors told Gehrig that he had what was known as amyotrophic lateral sclerosis (ALS). This big medical term means that a person who has this disease begins losing control of the nerves in their brain and spinal cord. If one can't control their muscles and movement in baseball, or most sports, then that player can't continue to play. Unfortunately, there is no cure for this disease. Shortly after his diagnosis, Gehrig announced that he would be retiring. The Yankees chose to honor Gehrig by making every July 4 Lou Gehrig Appreciation Day. On that day in 1939, Gehrig addressed all the fans in Yankee Stadium with these touching words:

> "For the past two weeks you have been reading about a bad break I got. Yet today I consider myself the luckiest man on the face of the earth. I have been in ballparks for seventeen years and have never received anything but kindness and encouragement from you fans. . . .
>
> "When everybody down to the groundskeepers and those boys in white coats remember you with trophies—that's something. . . . When you have a father and a mother who work all their lives so that you can have an education and build your body—it's a blessing. When you have a wife who has been a tower of strength and shown

> more courage than you dreamed existed—that's the finest I know.
>
> "So I close in saying that I might have had a bad break, but I've got an awful lot to live for."

Sadly, two years later Gehrig died. Today ALS is more commonly known as Lou Gehrig's disease. Since Gehrig was forced to quit at this point in his career, some people probably thought that this was the worst thing in the world to happen to him. However, Gehrig chose to look at the glass half full instead of half empty. Gehrig decided to highlight all the good things that had happened to him.

Life on this earth is short. Sports aren't just fun for the fans and the awards—they're also good witnessing opportunities. You may never get the chance to go on a mission trip or feed starving children, but you do have a chance to witness for God every time you put on a uniform.

Lou Gehrig's life made a positive impact on others. May your sports experience do the same.

I may have had a bad break,
but I've got an awful lot to live for.
—Lou Gehrig

Cheatin' Pete

In 1989, Cincinnati Reds player Pete Rose was accused of cheating in baseball. He cheated by betting on games that he was a part of. Now, cheating in general is wrong, but in baseball, it's really frowned on. Baseball players have very strict rules and don't like people who try to get around those rules. (Just look at how baseball treats all the players who use steroids.)

When Rose was caught cheating, he didn't want to bring any further shame to himself, so he accepted the penalty from the baseball commissioner. Sadly Rose was given a lifetime ban from baseball. Pete spent the next couple of decades hanging around baseball events declaring how sorry he was for what he had done. Since then he's done many public interviews asking for forgiveness—but never anything official. In early 2015, Rose tried again to get back into baseball. He sent official notice to the baseball commissioner requesting a pardon from the his lifetime ban. Unfortunately, at the time of this publication, Rose's request still has not been granted.

When Rose was caught cheating, he decided to accept whatever punishment came his way. Now, twenty-five years later, Rose feels that he should no longer be forced to suffer the consequences for what he did. What Rose doesn't seem to want to admit is that wrong is wrong. Although he has been forgiven for his actions, his punishment still stands. His lifetime ban excludes him from entering the National Baseball Hall of Fame. This is where all great baseball players are honored, and although Pete was a really good player, he's not allowed entry because of his lifetime ban. That's all it takes—doing one bad thing—to prevent a great player from making it into the Hall of Fame.

In a way, we're all kind of like Pete Rose. But there's one big difference: although we've done things that deserve punishment, when Jesus died for us He made sure that He would be blamed for our mistakes. Without His grace, we wouldn't be allowed into heaven. It doesn't matter if you've done one bad thing or a billion, sin is sin, and its punishment is death. Yikes! Aren't you grateful that Jesus made that sacrifice for us? Without it, we'd have no hope.

I actually feel sorry for Rose. All he wants is this one blemish from his career removed so that he can be allowed entry into baseball's Hall of Fame. But for Rose, there hasn't been any grace extended for his mistake, and it may never happen. For the rest of his life, Rose may have to carry the burden of his poor choices alone. As someone once said: "If you cheat, you're only cheating yourself."

The more people rationalize cheating, the more it becomes a culture of dishonesty. And that can become a vicious, downward cycle. Because suddenly, if everyone else is cheating, you feel a need to cheat, too.
–Stephen Covey

Warning Signs

You can't go very far without seeing a warning sign posted somewhere. There are red stop signs and yellow yield signs. There are signs that tell you to watch out for the slippery floor and fire alarm signs that tell you to pull them only in case of an emergency. These signs are placed in strategic positions to help us avoid danger. So what happens if these warning signs are ignored? People often get hurt.

Recently I read that there's something similar in baseball. If you look at the field, you'll notice that there is an orange-colored clay that borders the outfield. This section of the field is called the warning track, and it is part of every baseball field.

Major League Baseball players all know that when the texture underneath their feet changes from grass to clay, they have only about three steps before they run into the outfield wall. Despite this, players still frequently crash into the wall. Why does this happen if they have this "warning sign"?

Players choose to ignore the warning track in order to try to make a play. Sometimes it pays off, other times it doesn't. Very often when a player crashes into the wall they suffer an injury, some more gruesome than others. These injuries include broken arms, broken collarbones, and broken noses.

During the time when the Egyptians enslaved the Israelites, God sent Moses as a "warning sign" to Pharaoh. Through Moses, Pharaoh was warned that if he didn't release the Israelites, God would send plagues. These ten plagues included being overrun by frogs and locusts and parents losing their firstborn sons! Those are some serious warning signs, yet the Bible says that Pharaoh hardened his heart, which basically means that he ignored what God was saying to him.

God often sent warning signs in Bible times. But did you know that He gives us warning signs too? For example, God specifically warns us to be on the lookout for people claiming to be Him. He warns us that the way in which we judge others is how God will judge us. God also warns us that the world we live in won't be nice to us. But God doesn't leave us on that sad note. He also says that we shouldn't worry, because He has already conquered the world (John 16:33).

If we follow God's warning signs, it will help us avoid many things that otherwise might cause great injury to us, physically and spiritually. Pay attention to God's warning signs!

Make it so that your life can be a good example,
and not a horrible warning.
–Anonymous

A Matter of Perspective

I was watching a baseball game one day when something occurred to me: a strike in baseball is bad. If you get three strikes in baseball, you're out. However, getting a strike in bowling is good because it means you've knocked down all the pins. If you get three strikes in bowling, it's even better, because that means your score will be higher. There are some opposites that I noticed in other sports as well.

Having the lowest score in a hockey game is bad, because that means your team lost. But if you have the lowest score in a golf game, that means you won! In basketball it's not a good thing to carry the ball, but in football that's more than a good thing.

Doing something in one sport may mean something bad, but in another sport doing the same thing can mean something totally different. It just depends on what sport you're playing.

The best example of this in the Bible is the story of Joseph. At an early age he was sold into slavery by his brothers. From there he was thrown into prison, and that's probably the moment he felt at his lowest. He might have thought, *Why is all of this happening to me? What did I do to deserve this?* But the problem is that Joseph would have been looking at his story the wrong way. What may have seemed to be a long line of unfortunate events was actually being used by God to set Joseph up for a brighter future.

After Joseph went through all of that misery, he ended up being second-in-command of all Egypt. Being in this position allowed him to eventually help the very people who sold him into slavery in the first place! You can read more about Joseph, beginning in Genesis 37.

In John 16:33, Jesus told the disciples that in this world they would have trouble. That meant that there would be some bad days that they would have to deal with. And the same is true today. We all have to deal with bad days. They're frustrating and often discouraging, but there is a light at the end of the tunnel. Jesus finished His message to the disciples by also promising them that He has already overcome the world. James, a disciple of Jesus, supported this message when he told the people to "consider it all joy" whenever they faced bad days (James 1:2, NASB). Depending on how you look at it, bad days can be one of the worst or one of the best things that happened to you. It's all a matter of perspective.

Called Up

The year was 1944. Against the backdrop of World War II, American citizens were trying to maintain a somewhat normal life. Because of the war, most of the able-bodied men were in the military, which left some huge work gaps across a lot of industries, including sports. On June 10, 1944, the Cincinnati Reds baseball team was running low on players. Instead of forfeiting games, the Reds chose to let Joe Nuxhall pitch.

The special thing about Nuxhall was that he was only fifteen years old! Can you imagine pitching for a Major League Baseball team at such a young age? Nuxhall didn't have time to think about it, because the moment was here, and it was his time to show the world his talents. Nuxhall eventually went on to have an awesome career. He played for sixteen seasons, and during that time he was a two-time all-star, had a 3.9 ERA, and ended with a 135–117 record. Nuxhall is still the youngest player to have pitched in a major league game. After his playing days were over, Nuxhall went on to be a broadcaster for thirty-seven years.

Having such a long career is often an indication of how good you are at something. More important, being asked to take part in something from a young age is an honor. There was also a young guy in the Bible who was called up to be a part of something great—Josiah. After his father was assassinated, Josiah was crowned king of Judah at eight years old. As king, Josiah did many great things for Judah, including restoring many of Moses' laws. King Josiah went on to reign for thirty-one years.

From Joe Nuxhall to King Josiah, you're never too young to take a leadership position. I remember being asked in sixth grade to play on the high school basketball team. It was nerve-racking, but I realized that even though I was young, I was being asked to play because I was good enough and they needed me. To this day, I still play basketball, and I also use what I've learned to help share my experiences when I write.

In life there may come a time you're asked to do something that you feel someone older should do. Whether that's reading a Bible text up front at church or playing on a high school team even though you're not in high school yet, embrace the challenge! Each of us has been placed in a position to better help explain God's character of love. When that moment comes, don't be nervous. Just do what you've been doing, and the rest will take care of itself.

Age is no barrier. It's a limitation you put on your mind.
—Jackie Joyner-Kersee

Basketball

Taming the Fire

On December 9, 1977, the Los Angeles Lakers' Kermit Washington was involved in a scuffle at midcourt with one of the players from the Houston Rockets. Rudy Tomjanovich, the captain of the Rockets, ran over to the scuffle to see what was happening. Washington thought Tomjanovich was coming over to fight him, so Washington punched Tomjanovich in the face. The repercussions of that action have haunted Washington all his life.

The details are a bit gory, but Washington hit Tomjanovich so hard that spinal fluid started leaking into Tomjanovich's mouth. People describe hearing the hit and thinking that the scoreboard had fallen from the ceiling. (Stop and think about that. Do you know how loud that would sound?) Washington has since admitted that he regrets what he did and that he wishes he could go back in time to change the outcome. (Tomjanovich had to undergo reconstructive surgery.)

Have you ever done something while competing and then later wished you could take it back? I certainly have said or done some things while competing that I shouldn't have done. They were nothing as serious as making someone taste spinal fluid, but they definitely weren't Christlike either. Fortunately, to my knowledge, the things I did never had a lasting effect. Unfortunately for Moses in the Bible, his actions cost him dearly.

Now, Moses wasn't exactly competing in the traditional sense of the word, but he was fighting for the hearts of the Israelites. Once again the children of Israel were complaining, and they wanted water. The Lord met with Moses and told him to speak to the rock and water would come out of it. However, in his anger, Moses struck the rock with his stick not once but twice! Then he said, "Must we bring water for you out of this rock?" (Numbers 20:10, NKJV). He made it sound like he and Aaron were going to work a miracle, not God. Poor Moses. Because of his actions, the Lord told Moses that he wouldn't be able to enter the Promised Land.

I bet Moses wished he could take those words and actions back. When we do things in anger, it almost never turns out well. Think about all the sporting events in which someone lost their cool. There's the 2004 brawl between the Indiana Pacers and the Detroit Pistons; World Cup 2006, when Zinedine Zidane head-butted a player in the chest and was red-carded from the game; Mike Tyson biting Evander Holyfield's ear off. As far as I know, none of these situations worked out well.

The next time you feel yourself getting heated about a bad call or the next time a player is purposely trying to rile you up, walk away. I know it may be hard, but that's the best thing you can do, because in that moment when your temper flares, you might do something you wish you hadn't. Always remember: it's just a game!

A quick temper will make a fool of you soon enough.
—Bruce Lee

That's the Spirit!

Why is this even called an award? I thought snidely as I turned the Spirit Award over in my hands. Who wants an award for losing?

It was award night at the annual Southwestern Adventist University basketball tournament. That year my team "won" the Spirit Award. To make matters worse, all team members had to get up on stage and accept the trophy as a team. Ugh. Not only did my team not place, but we also had to accept this rinky-dink award as a consolation.

I felt that as long as they were awarding kindness, they might as well pass out other awards too. Why not create the Travel Warrior Award for the team who came the farthest to the tournament or the Medic Award for the team who got the most injuries? Silly? Perhaps, but that's exactly how I felt about the Spirit Award.

Helping someone up after a fall and winning respectfully are things I assumed everyone did. Well, we all know what they say about assuming; don't do it. I eventually realized that some players don't know how to be the "good Samaritan" in the game.

By now you should all know the parable of the good Samaritan. It showed how one person can make a difference. Other people had the opportunity to help the injured man and didn't, but the good Samaritan acted on his conscience. The Bible says that the Samaritan "bandaged his wounds, pouring on oil" (Luke 10:34, NKJV). Then the Samaritan literally went the extra mile by putting the man on his donkey and taking him to an inn. He also took care of the bill. Wow!

What makes the story even more special is that the man he helped was Jewish. Back then Jews and Samaritans didn't hang out together because they didn't like each other. See the correlation to sports?

Now I'm not saying that teams should strive solely to win the Spirit Award. Teams don't travel hundreds of miles to get recognized for their kindness. Teams come to win. However, on the chance that your team doesn't win it all, getting the Spirit Award isn't that bad. Often good actions and deeds go unrewarded. So the next time someone wants to recognize you or your team for its kindness, just smile and accept the compliment.

For when the One Great Scorer comes to mark against your name, He writes–not that you won or lost–but how you played the Game.
–Grantland Rice

The Crying Champion

Wow.

That was the thought that entered my head the first time I saw Michael Jordan cry. It was a moment that will stick with me forever. On the hardwood Jordan was unstoppable, unguardable, and (for those who remember) "unbeatabull." The only thing he hadn't done yet was win a championship. In his mind, all of his other accomplishments seemed pointless without that one.

Jordan was a machine of a player who showed no remorse for punishing opponents. (An opponent once told reporters that he didn't bring his family to the game when he played against Jordan.) But when Jordan finally won his first championship, he cried. Despite all the flashing cameras and celebration around him, he held that trophy in his hands and cried. I couldn't believe it. At that point, for a brief second, Jordan was human.

A similar thought process must have been running through people's minds when they first saw Jesus cry. Most of us know that John 11:35 is the shortest verse in the Bible, but it probably most fully describes Jesus' character. Up until that point Jesus had shown compassion to others and performed miracles. However, we get to see another side of Jesus at Lazarus's tomb. When Jesus arrived, He saw all the heartache that death caused, and He remembered that this wasn't a part of the original plan. He saw all the mourners who had gathered to remember His friend, and He must have literally felt all the sadness from everyone in that place. Jesus' heart was heavy, so He wept. This act showed everyone that He wasn't just God among humans–but an actual human with real emotions.

I once told one of the basketball players I coached, "Never let them see you cry." I gave that advice after a tough loss to a rival team. As the final buzzer sounded, this guy immediately collapsed to the floor and cried. I walked over to him and mistakenly gave him the right advice at the wrong time. At the time I didn't want our rivals thinking he was weak, but I should've been more compassionate toward his feelings. Hey, even coaches make mistakes!

It's OK to cry, win or lose. It shows that you've given 100 percent and then some to what you believe in. Never let anyone take that passion away from you. So this one is for you, "Drew," wherever you are.

Sport is where an entire life can be compressed into a few hours. Where the emotions of a lifetime can be felt on the acre or two of ground.
—George A. Sheehan

Know Your Role

I knew a guy in high school who was six feet four and wanted to do nothing but shoot threes and dunk the ball. (OK, I'm the guy.) Now, I was a decent enough three-point shooter, but there were other people on our team who did it better. However, I didn't let the norms of basketball hold me back. When I was in games, I would always drift toward the three-point line just to shoot. Every once in a while I'd make it, but for the most part I would miss.

One day my coach sat me down and asked me why I wanted to shoot threes. "Because I can," came the natural response. That's when my coach taught me the dynamics of a team. *Dynamics* is just a big word that means "how things work." Remember when I said that I was six feet four? The next-tallest person on our team was five feet eleven, and the other team members were drastically shorter. My coach explained that although I could shoot threes, I would better serve my team if I were closer to the basket. And suddenly the light bulb switched on.

Everybody on our team was there for a reason. We had a good ball handler, good rebounders, three-point specialists, and so on. I was the tallest guy on the team, and I didn't want to fill the position that helped my team the most. It's not that I couldn't shoot threes in a game, but my coach wanted me in my natural position first.

On any team there are different but important parts to play. A basketball team wouldn't function well if the center wanted to play the point guard position. How good would a baseball team be if the pitcher wanted to play shortstop?

In 1 Corinthians 12:12–27 Jesus, speaking through Paul, makes this really cool metaphor (comparison) that describes the church as a literal body. He stresses how important it is for each body part to do its job, just like people in His church. All for one and one for all.

What if your brain had a conference and told certain parts of your body that they were fired? "Hey, fingernails, we don't need you anymore. Budget cuts."

Crazy, right? We need all the parts of our body so that it can function properly. Each part has its specific role. If one part stops working, the entire body suffers. The same thing applies to our church "team." Each position (junior deacon, pastor, VBS leader, missionary, and so on) is there for a reason. Once you've been assigned a position, play it to your fullest potential! Whether people realize it or not, all positions are important. Without all the players, it's hard to have a winning team.

I am a member of a team, and I rely on the team,
I defer to it and sacrifice for it, because the team,
not the individual, is the ultimate champion.
—Mia Hamm

The Secret of the High Five

A while back I heard that babies who are touched frequently are healthier than those who aren't. Sounds weird, doesn't it? But there are tons of research reports about it. Scientists discovered that just a simple, caring touch stimulates growth in the body, changes behavior, and even enhances self-esteem!*

So what do babies have to do with the Sports Zone? How about this: I'm sure plenty of you sports junkies watched at least one game of the 2011 NBA Finals. Just in case you've forgotten, let me refresh your memory. The Dallas Mavericks beat the Miami Heat. That season Dwyane Wade, LeBron James, and Chris Bosh had all teamed up to make kind of a superteam. Many sports analysts reported that if Miami reached the finals, they would win on talent alone. The one thing that they forgot about was chemistry. The Dallas players overcame many obstacles and hurdles that year, and as a result, they were a much closer team than Miami.

After three games, *The Wall Street Journal* printed an article that recorded–get this–how many times teammates gave each other positive physical interaction (PPI). That's just the fancy way of saying a high five here, a chest bump there, or maybe even a hug. How did both teams do?

Dallas crushed Miami in PPI. Dallas' Tyson Chandler was a high-five machine and led all the players with ninety. Wow, that's a lot of high fives! The article went on to state that high fives aren't necessarily the secret to winning. If that were the case, I think all teams would make it mandatory to give at least ten high fives during each game.

The study was simply revealing that the more PPI on a team, the more positive chemistry they're likely to have.†

---

* Maria Konnikova, "The Power of Touch," *The New Yorker*, March 4, 2015, https://www.newyorker.com/science/maria-konnikova/power-touch.

† Scott Cacciola, "Dallas's Secret Weapon:: High Fives," *The Wall Street Journal*, June 9, 2011, https://www.wsj.com/articles/SB10001424052702304392704576373641168929846.

In our super technological world of texting and online gaming, when's the last time you showed someone PPI? More important, how many times do you think Jesus did it? PPI allows us to make a powerful connection with someone, so give it a try.

Too often we underestimate the power of a touch, a smile, a kind word, a listening ear, an honest compliment, or the smallest act of caring, all of which have the potential to turn a life around.
—Leo Buscaglia

What's the Point of—?

"Practice?" Allen Iverson asked in disbelief. "We're talking about practice."

Those words are now infamous in the halls of basketball history. It was 2002, and the Philadelphia 76ers had just been defeated in the first round of the NBA playoffs. During a press conference after the final game, 76ers Coach Larry Brown criticized Iverson for missing team practices.

Shortly afterward, a reporter asked Iverson to respond to his coach's comment, and Iverson decided to let the media know exactly how he felt. For the next two minutes he went on a rant in which he frustratedly said the word "practice" more than twenty times! His complaint was that if he never missed an official game and always played his hardest, then what was the point of practice?

In a last-ditch effort to help Iverson clarify his thoughts, a different reporter asked him, "Is it possible that if you practiced, you would make your teammates better?"

To this Iverson responded (with an expletive), "How . . . can I make my teammates better by practicing?"

The echo of his response stunned the room of reporters and lingered in the air like a foul stench. I'm sure many of them were thinking, *Did he really just say that?* How could Iverson, Philadelphia's franchise player, not understand the value of practice?

For the remainder of his career in the NBA, Iverson accomplished many great personal stats but never really grasped the value of practice. Practice is more than just showing up to do drills and work on plays—it's a time to connect with your teammates in friendship and hard work. Whether I'm coaching or playing, I love going to practice. Some of the best memories are made there. Practice allows me to see what my weaknesses are and also understand my teammates' weaknesses. In practice, we grow as a team and become stronger. It's called *synergy*. None of that would be possible if I skipped out on practice.

In my opinion, skipping out on practice is just like not going to church. Sometimes church is viewed as a place where you get *Guide* magazines and then read them until the service is over. Sorry to disappoint you, but church has a lot more value than that. Church is a place for you to figure out your spiritual weaknesses. It's also a time to learn something new so that you can add it to your spiritual arsenal, because honestly, we all need to step up our game. Sin is out there, and guess what: it never takes a day off. Just remember that. It's church, y'all—I'm talking about church.

When you are not practicing, remember, someone somewhere is practicing, and when you meet him, he will win.
—Ed Macauley

The Heart of Basketball

Ever since the addition of the shot clock there has been a rift between basketball fans. On one side, fans reason that the shot clock speeds up the game and makes it more interesting to watch. I'll call these fans "modernists." On the other hand, some fans think that the shot clock rushes the natural flow of the game. They feel that this has ruined the heart of basketball. I'll call these fans "purists," since they want the game to stay pure.

Basketball purists are an intriguing group. They liked the

game with its original thirteen rules. They think that by adding things such as a shot clock, a three-point line, and even crossover dribbles, their sacred game has been destroyed.

I don't necessarily agree with the purists, but I understand their concerns. In my opinion, the NBA has already become less team-oriented and more about showmanship. Sports media outlets such as ESPN highlight dunks and showboating over solid screens and box-outs. As a result we've become more focused on raw athletic ability rather than sound fundamentals.

Although basketball isn't what it used to be, I believe the game has changed for the better. Various NBA commissioners have made basketball more challenging by adjusting the rules, but the goal is still the same: score more points than your opponent.

So which side is right?

In the Bible, Paul faced a similar dilemma. The disciples had been charged with taking the gospel to the world. Paul had accepted the challenge and run with it. In 1 Corinthians 9:22, he stated that he'd become "all things to all men" (NKJV). He'd learned how to effectively spread God's Word to different groups, making it meaningful to them without changing the core of the message.

Many people disagreed with Paul's approach. They felt that he wasn't following the original rules set by God. They needn't have worried, because Paul knew that there were limits to his method and that above all he was still bound by "the law of Christ" (verse 21, NASB). As long as he stayed within those boundaries, though, he had tremendous freedom.

Whether in playing basketball or sharing the gospel, sometimes there is no "right" side. God created us all as unique individuals. Naturally, we will each have a different view on how the game should be played or the gospel should be shared. The important thing is that the heart of basketball—and the gospel—remains untouched.

"Though I am free and belong to no one, I have made myself a slave to everyone, to win as many as possible. . . . I do all this for

the sake of the gospel, that I may share in its blessings."
—1 Corinthians 9:19, 23, NIV

Be Like Michael

Years ago Gatorade released a Michael Jordan commercial that is still ingrained in people's minds. The commercial depicted men, women, and children trying to imitate Jordan's greatest in-game moves. At the end the commercial said: "Be like Mike. Drink Gatorade." It wasn't exactly subtle; Gatorade could help you be like Michael Jordan.

The reason Gatorade chose the "be like Mike" theme is that he was quickly becoming the dominant athlete in basketball. With every game he played after his first championship, he looked more and more unstoppable. Michael Jordan wasn't the blueprint for what every person should be but rather an exceptional basketball player to emulate.

In 1 Corinthians 11:1, Paul encourages Christians to be like him. Instead of making a commercial, he handwrote letters to his audience. In those letters, he urged people to be like him—without his flaws. Paul knew that he was imperfect, but his heart was in the right place. He also knew that Christianity was more about "being" than "acting." Sometimes Christians fall into the trap of doing and saying all the right things but not being pure on the inside.

As we continue to grow as Christians, it's important to remember why we are trying to be like Jesus, who is also known as Michael (Revelation 12:7). It's not so that we can show everyone what a great Christian we are but to show them that they can also become like Christ.

The Gatorade commercial didn't want you to be Michael Jordan. They knew that not everyone was going to grow up to be six feet six and 220 pounds, and even if they did, that didn't mean they'd be able to do everything Jordan could do. They wanted people to strive to be the best basketball player ever. Paul didn't want people to be him either; he wanted people to follow his example to be the best Christian they could possibly be.

The question you need to ask yourself every day is, Who am I trying to be like?

Sometimes I dream, that he is me
You've got to see, that's how I dream to be
I dream I move, I dream I groove
Like Mike, if I could be like Mike
Again I try, just need to fly
For just one day, if I could be that way
I dream I move, I dream I groove
Like Mike, if I could be like Mike

To the weak I became weak, to win the weak. I have become all things to all people so that by all possible means I might save some. I do all this for the sake of the gospel, that I may share in its blessings.
—1 Corinthians 9:22, 23, NIV

The Power of Habit

"Don't ever underestimate the heart of a champion!" Coach Rudy Tomjanovich proclaimed after his Houston Rockets team overcame near impossible odds to win the 1994–1995 NBA championship. After previously winning the title in the 1993–1994 season, the Rockets entered the playoffs the next season as the sixth seed out of eight in the Western Conference. There were no buzzer-beating shots or close games, but the Rockets simply kept playing hard and eventually won their second championship. The Rockets refused to lose—it's that simple.

Champions come in all shapes and sizes, but the heart of a champion will always look the same. I believe that a champion's heart is made from a drop of courage, an ounce of inspiration, and a dash of determination. It's one thing to win, but it's something completely different to be known for winning. Somehow champions find ways to overcome the odds because they have made a habit of winning.

I recently read a book that discusses habits. The book talks about how the brain tries to form routines—habits—so that it can conserve energy. For instance, every Sabbath morning, many Seventh-day Adventists have formed the habit of going to church. It's been so instilled in our brains that it can feel strange if you aren't in church that day. As for champions, they have formed the habit of winning. They automatically do all the small things that need to be done in order to win. Whether it's diving on the floor for a loose ball, making an unbelievable catch, or hitting a home run, champions find a way to win because that's what they're used to doing. That's not to say that champions never lose; it simply means that they win more times than the average person.

The Bible is full of wisdom and guidance, and the more time we devote to reading and studying its pages, the more natural and helpful it will become to our lives. It will soon be a habit that goes a long way toward building a character that pleases God. Sure, our ultimate motivation to devote time to studying God's Word is to know its Author better. Yet if we begin the habit of reading the Bible and following its wisdom, good things will happen in our hearts. We might even become champions for God.

We are what we repeatedly do. Excellence, then, is not an act but a habit.
—Will Durant

The Pivot

Imagine you're playing a game of basketball (or "netball" for my Euro-savvy readers). You have the ball and cannot move forward at all because that would be traveling, a violation. Your only option is to pass the ball to one of your teammates, but there is a pesky defender in front of you, making it hard to pass. What should you do?

Pivot.

The pivot move is used in basketball, netball, and other sports. This move requires a player to be at a standstill. Then, while keeping one foot firmly planted to the ground, the player must use their other leg to swing in either a clockwise or counter-clockwise motion. Pivoting is a great move because it allows the player to get a better angle on a tough situation. I've seen some of the more experienced players in the NBA specialize in this move. They will frequently use it to make extraordinary passes or shots. (Pay close attention to the next basketball game you watch and see how many times you can spot a pivot.)

A good example of a "life pivot" is the apostle Paul. Early in life Paul (or Saul, as he was known then) made it his business to persecute Christians ruthlessly. You can read the details of the story in Acts 9. Basically, when Saul was on his way to Damascus to find more Christians to persecute, God confronted him. He spoke to Saul and asked him, "Why do you persecute me?" (verse 4, NIV).

Saul was dumbfounded.

God blinded Saul and told him to meet with Ananias before he could be healed.

Eventually he was healed, and Saul (a Jewish name) became Paul (a Roman name). Apparently Paul wanted to make a fresh start as a Christian, and that included a name change. Paul went from persecuting Christians to becoming a Christian leader. What a pivot!

Satan sometimes acts like that pesky defender in front of you on a basketball court. He makes it very hard for you to see the clear path. This is the point where you have to pivot. Is there something that you're doing in your life right now that you know isn't good? Would you like to pivot out of that behavior? Ask God for help, and He will send the Holy Spirit to guide you. Psalm 55:22 says: "Cast your cares on the LORD and he will sustain you" (NIV).

When it comes to having Jesus as a teammate, there's no way you will lose.

Whenever you find yourself in a [bad] situation . . . find a "pivot point" that will allow you to pivot away from the source of your problems.
–Chris Lehane

Custom-Made Success

Once during a 2013 Indiana Pacers practice session, a ball careened off the rim and rolled over to the team president and former NBA great, Larry Bird. When the ball stopped at his feet, the fifty-six-year-old Bird picked up the ball and rolled up his sleeves.

The Pacer team watched. Bird stepped a little beyond the three-point line and shot.

Swoosh!

Someone must have rebounded the ball and given it back to him, because Bird repeated his shot and got nothing but net.

Bird continued to shoot and made fifteen three-pointers in a row! After the fifteenth shot, Bird threw the ball to one of the Pacers' players and walked out of the gym without saying a word.

Bird hasn't played professional basketball since 1992. So how was he able to make so many shots in a row? To answer that question, we need to learn about how Bird got so good in the first place.

The former basketball star's work ethic is legendary. When he played professionally, he was the first one in the gym and the last one to leave. After practice, Bird wouldn't leave the gym until he made ten perfect free throws in a row. By perfect, I mean that the ball couldn't hit any part of the rim, and the net had to splash upward as the ball passed through. Bird would spend hours in the gym until he achieved his goal. You could say that it was his custom.

When people read about Jesus' life, they often wonder about the secret of His spiritual strength. The Bible tells us that "Jesus often withdrew to lonely places and prayed" (Luke 5:16, NIV). The verse is short, but it's important because it tells us that this was our Savior's custom.

Jesus often retreated to a quiet place to get closer to His

Father. This is why, even when Jesus was just twelve years old, the adults in the temple courts marveled at His knowledge of the Scriptures (see Luke 2:47). This is also why people flocked to Jesus when He was out in public. People just wanted to learn from Him.

If you want to be successful in anything, you must be willing to start with the small things. Maybe it's as easy as staying an extra hour for practice. Maybe it's something a little more challenging, such as studying a bit more for school. Or maybe it's as hard as getting up earlier to have personal devotions. In order to be successful, there must be some sacrifice on your part. Figure out what you need to do to be successful, and make it your custom.

Working hard becomes a habit, a serious kind of fun. You get self-satisfaction from pushing yourself to the limit, knowing that all the effort is going to pay off.
—Mary Lou Retton

Keep On Shooting

It was a sad time in the land of Israel. God's chosen people were being oppressed by the king of Aram. To make matters worse, God's prophet Elisha was very ill. During his last days, Elisha was visited by Jehoash, Israel's king. King Jehoash wept over Elisha, for he knew that Elisha would not be alive much longer. Seeing his distress, Elisha decided to bless Jehoash.

Elisha told Jehoash to get a bow and some arrows. It was a strange request, but Jehoash did it anyway. Then Elisha told him to put his hands on the bow, which Jehoash also did. Next Elisha put his hands on top of Jehoash's hands. The prophet told Jehoash to open the east window and shoot an arrow out of it. Jehoash did this. As Bible scholar Matthew Henry wrote, "The trembling hands of a dying prophet . . . gave this arrow more force than the hands of the king in his full strength."*

Finally Elisha instructed Jehoash to take more arrows and strike the ground. Again, Jehoash didn't really know where this was going, but the Bible says he struck the ground with three arrows and then stopped.

At this, Elisha became upset with Jehoash. "You should have struck the ground five or six times; then you would have defeated Aram and completely destroyed it. But now you will defeat it only three times" (2 Kings 13:19, NIV). And true to Elisha's word, Jehoash was able to overthrow Aram only three times in the effort to recapture the cities of Israel.

As a coach, I remember a time after basketball practice when a player came over and asked me how he could improve his game. I told him to shoot free throws. The player took the ball, shot about ten times, and then went on to shoot random jump shots. I shook my head because when I told the player to shoot free throws, I wanted him to shoot maybe a hundred times. Shooting ten times is a warm-up. Shooting a hundred times creates muscle memory, which leads to improved shooting accuracy. That player's meager effort showed me that he wasn't giving it his all.

What I understand from the story of Jehoash and Elisha is that if someone whom you consider wise tells you to do something, do it until it becomes second nature. It's like when Jesus said to forgive "seventy-seven times" (Matthew 18:22, NIV). He didn't mean you should forgive someone only up to seventy-seven times and then stop. He meant that we should to do it until it becomes second nature.

No matter what you want to be good at in life, the point is to keep practicing. Do something until you don't even realize you're doing it anymore. The battles you fight now contribute to the victories you'll have later.

---

* "2 Kings 13," *Matthew Henry's Complete Commentary on the Bible*, StudyLight.org, accessed March 6, 2019, https://www.studylight.org/commentaries/mhm/2-kings-13.html.

Never stop learning, because life never stops teaching.
—Anonymous

Fading Glory

In 2 Kings 20, we find out that King Hezekiah is deathly sick. The king had lived a good life up until his illness, and he'd done what was right in the eyes of the Lord. It's safe to say that God thought very highly of him. Unfortunately, the prophet Isaiah came to him with a message from God, saying, "Put your house in order, because you are going to die; you will not recover" (verse 1, NIV). Upon hearing this, Hezekiah cried out to God for healing, and God granted him fifteen extra years of life!

God also granted him a sign that he had asked for Babylonians who saw this sign came to see King Hezekiah in awe.*

King Hezekiah then showed them everything in his entire kingdom. He showed them his land, livestock, grains, treasures, and even his palace. After the visitors had seen everything in King Hezekiah's kingdom, they left for home. And that's when Isaiah came back around.

He asked Hezekiah what he had shown the visitors. Hezekiah said that he had shown them everything in his palace. At this point, I feel that Isaiah shook his head and with a sigh said, "There will come a time when everything in your palace will be carried off to Babylon. And your descendants, even some of your own children, will be eunuchs in the palace of the Babylonian king" (see verses 16–18).

That's a tough lesson to learn. Everything that Hezekiah and his ancestors had worked for was soon to be gone, all because Hezekiah forgot to acknowledge the God who gave him those things. So why am I telling you this?

I remember my high school basketball glory days, which were

---

* See Ellen G. White, *Prophets and Kings*, pp. 342–346 for the whole story.

not so long ago. In my senior year, I averaged twenty points, fourteen rebounds, and six blocks per game! At the end of the season I was named the best center in the league, which means that I was mentioned alongside other high school seniors at the time, including Roy Hibbert, Ty Lawson, Jeff Green, Rudy Gay, and Kevin Durant! Those players all went on to play in the NBA.

But think about it—none of you knew that about me. Which means that most people don't remember all the hard work I did on the court. But what people do remember is my character. I didn't make the same mistake that Hezekiah did. I understood that my talents on the court were only a backdrop for how God really wanted to use me. And now I get to share my stories and life lessons with readers, including you, all over the world. So don't take sports so seriously! Remember, if you are good at something, it's just the setting for how God truly wants to use you.

On the field I'm trying to play for the glory of God. . . . More than just winning or losing, I think He cares about where our hearts are when we're playing.
—Tim Tebow

Goals Don't Change

Each new NBA season begins with high hopes for all teams, but things don't always go as planned. The Boston Celtics learned that at the beginning of the 2017–2018 NBA season. During the off-season the Celtics made two huge moves by getting Gordon Hayward and Kyrie Irving to play for them. Adding to the drama, Irving was traded from his former team, whom they happened to be playing against on opening night. The atmosphere was electric! Each team wanted to prove that they had the better team.

About five minutes into the first quarter, Hayward jumped up for an alley-oop to dunk the ball, but the pass was broken up by the defense. As Hayward came down, he landed awkwardly on his foot. I'll spare you the gruesome details, but he ended up breaking his shinbone and dislocating his ankle. This injury kept him from playing the rest of the season.

Many connected with the NBA thought this meant that the Celtics wouldn't perform well that season, but this is where Celtics' guard Shane Larkin stepped in to voice his opinion. In an interview he was asked if the expectations for the Celtics' season had changed now that they wouldn't have Hayward.

Larkin responded that the goal is still the same; the team is here to win a championship. He went on to explain that although they had lost one member of the team for a season, this just meant that everyone else on the team had to step up. It would be tough but not impossible.

In the Bible, there was also a group of men who had high expectations for their season. The disciples had followed Jesus and His principles, and each had an idea of how Jesus was going to take over the world. Their high expectations made them think that Jesus would act like an earthly king. So when Jesus told them that He was going to be crucified, and then it actually happened, the disciples were worried and confused.

If Jesus died, how could He conquer the world? Had they put their trust in the right person? In John 16:16–33, Jesus comes back to the disciples to comfort them. In verse 20, He tells them that they will weep while the world rejoices, but their grief will turn into joy. And in verse 33, He tells them that although they will experience trouble, they should be of good cheer, because He has overcome the world.

In both examples, team members had to deal with losing a leader. But in both cases, the message was the same: the goal doesn't change because of the circumstances. Our goal is to help others know about God's love. The world will make it tough on us, but it's not impossible.

In times of difficulty, those brave enough to
stay the course will be victors in the end.
—Bo Schembechler

Running

Racing Without Rules

"I'm fast, Uncle!" my five-year-old niece claimed.

Obviously we had to race. We chose a starting place and an ending, but then I switched it up on her.

"Ready, set . . . " I said, but I never said "go" because I started running on the word *set*. I thought it was funny, but my niece was not amused. She was upset because I hadn't played by the rules.

Rules are important because they help bring structure to our pursuits. Every sport you can think of has rules. Let's take the example of the race with my niece and completely remove the rules. The basic rules of a race are picking a starting point, picking an ending point, and deciding when to start racing. Without rules my niece and I aren't racing anymore—we're just running around. Without rules, the race has no purpose.

Let's break it down a little further. A last-second shot in basketball is spectacular only because of the rules of the game. Think about it: a shot is still a shot. If there were more time on the clock, making the shot wouldn't be that big of a deal. Or if there were no clock at all, it wouldn't even matter. However, because the rules state that you have only a certain amount of time before the game is finished, the fact that a player made a last-second shot within regulation time makes it incredible. That's really what sports are about: doing relatively simple things under a defined set of rules. Without those rules, you're just doing simple things. Rules make sports purposeful.

Rules exist beyond the sports world, of course, including laws that we are wise to obey. Otherwise we get in trouble for not following them.

God set up rules for us as Christians to follow as well. Living by them gives us a sense of direction and purpose. We want to live by these rules because we love God, and this is what He asks of us. As a bonus, by following these rules we get the ultimate reward of eternal life with Him in heaven. (Talk about an incentive contract!) If God didn't give us rules to live by, then we would be living without purpose. Without rules, also known as structure, there is no purpose to anything.

Ask yourself why you are a Christian. What are the rules for following Christ? By answering these questions, you can live your life with purpose. Otherwise, you may just be running around aimlessly, the way my niece and I were.

You have to learn the rules of the game.
And then you have to play better than anyone else.
—Albert Einstein

The ~~Winner~~ Cheater Is . . .

In April 2015, Kendall Schler participated in a marathon (a marathon is 26.2 miles long) in St. Louis. This event wasn't nationally televised, but if Schler ran a good time in this marathon, she would qualify for the prestigious Boston Marathon. The winner of the St. Louis marathon would win some money and also have their photo taken with Olympic gold medalist Jackie Joyner-Kersee.

Apparently Schler registered for the race like everyone else but then waited and slipped in shortly before the finish line. As soon as she crossed the finish line and came in first place, race officials became suspicious. Several things didn't add up. For one thing, she wasn't sweating as hard as the other runners, nor did she exhibit the form of an elite runner. She also didn't register at time intervals along the race, meaning that there was a possibility that she cheated. She was also wearing her race bib in the wrong place, and she came in alone without the bicyclist who rides beside the leader. But it got even worse for Schler.

Race officials looked through photos and could not find a single picture of her during the middle of the race! They went even further by reviewing her race time in the 2014 marathon. The conclusion was that she cheated in that race as well. As a result Schler was disqualified from both races, and her invitation to run in the Boston Marathon was taken back. At the end Schler didn't deny that she cheated. The only thing she wanted to know was if she could run in the Boston Marathon!

I once thought about cheating when I had to run a mile for PE class. We had to run two and a half laps around a neighborhood where there were many opportunities to cheat. However, I quickly ignored that thought and ran the full mile. I ended up not placing first, but still ran a good time. Mostly I was just happy that I hadn't cheated.

Temptations in life are unavoidable; even Jesus faced them. After His "marathon" in the wilderness, Jesus was very tired and hungry. Spending forty days in intense spiritual training is a grueling process, and that's when Satan tried to tempt Him. The devil came at Jesus from all angles and made very compelling reasons for submitting to him. Thankfully, Jesus resisted. He knew that grace for humanity was at stake if He cheated.

If I had cheated, the consequences would not have been as dire, but I knew that I'd be a stronger runner for having run the entire race. Remember that God won't allow you to be tempted beyond what you can bear (1 Corinthians 10:13). Use this encouragement to help you overcome the unavoidable temptations in life.

Temptations when we meet them at first, are as the lion that roared upon Samson; but if we overcome them, the next time we see them we shall find a nest of honey within them.
—John Bunyan

Comeback Stories

In my lifetime I've been blessed to see some awesome comebacks by sports teams. It's very exciting to witness, especially if the team that you're rooting for is losing but then wins the game. The most memorable comebacks I've seen are in basketball. I remember Tracy McGrady scoring 13 points in 33 seconds; Derek Fisher making the game-winning shot with .4 seconds left; Kris Jenkins's three-point shot to win a national title; and, more recently, Stephen Curry drilling a more than thirty-foot shot to beat the Oklahoma City Thunder.

If you were rooting for the team that won, then you'll remember that game favorably down to the very last detail. But what if you were rooting for the other team? You wouldn't think these were good games at all. In fact, you'd probably think it was unfair that your team lost. For a long time that's how I felt about the parable of the vineyard workers.

In Matthew 20:1–16, Jesus wanted the crowd to understand who would be able to enter the kingdom of heaven. He decided to tell them a parable. Jesus explained that early one morning a vineyard owner went out and hired workers. He told them that they would be paid at the end of the day. He then hired more workers at midday, afternoon, and even in the evening right before the day was over. When it came time to pay everyone, the landowner paid all of them the same wage. Naturally, the workers who were hired in the morning complained. It wasn't fair that they had worked all day but were paid the same as the workers who were hired in the evening. And for a long time I agreed with them. I missed the point.

I had compared the story to a bunch of marathon runners who all finished at different times but all got a first-place trophy. Seems unfair, right? So why would God do it that way? But over the years, as I kept rereading the story, I realized that it wasn't really about work and wages but rather one's salvation. Imagine your life as a game against the enemy. For some of us, we're able to execute the right game plan (choosing to accept Jesus and following His plan for our lives) and take a big lead early on. Others, who don't have a good game plan, quickly fall behind on the scoreboard. But just as the workers who were hired in the evening and were paid the same as everyone else, God wants everyone who is losing to the enemy to have a comeback. He wants all of us to be in heaven with Him; whether you accept that earlier or later is up to you. But do yourself a favor by getting an early lead in the game.

Starting strong is good. Finishing strong is epic.
–Robin Sharma

Curling

Waymakers

Admittedly I haven't seen many curling games. But the strategy behind the sport fascinates me. Often called "chess on ice," curling is a game in which two teams of four try to throw their stones into the center of the target. The target, also known as the house, is on one end of a big sheet of ice about 15 feet across and 150 feet long. The teams will take turns sliding their stones down the ice toward the house.

This is where the true strategy of the game comes in. While the stone is sliding down the ice toward the house, the player is hoping to knock the opposing team's stones out of the way. Normally, a stone couldn't slide down a 150-foot sheet of ice with just one push and stop where the team wants it to, but that's where the sweepers are introduced.

A sweeper's job is to prepare the way for the stone. As the stone slides down the ice, the sweepers sweep the ice directly in front of the stone. By sweeping the ice in front of the stone, sweepers reduce the friction. If there's too much friction, the stone can't go in a straight line, and it will begin to curve. The more the sweepers sweep, the straighter the stone will travel. It's the sweepers' job to prepare the way for the stone so that it can travel as far and as straight as possible.

Now, this may sound crazy, but I found a "sweeper" in the Bible. In Matthew 3, there's this fellow named John the Baptist. And verse 3 describes John's job by saying that he is to "prepare the way for the Lord, make straight paths for him" (NIV). God is also known as the Rock (not the actor). So if John has to prepare the way for Him, he's got to be a sweeper, right? While it's not John's official title, I think it matches perfectly. But John isn't the only sweeper. Did you know that that is your job too?

God has an awesome message of love that He wants to share with the whole world. Unfortunately there's a lot of friction in front of that message so it can't go as far and as straight as it needs to. Friction can occur when people hate one another. This is where you and I come in. It's up to us to help reduce that friction by being kind to one another and being good representatives of that message. It's always a tough job, but if we sweep early and often, the message can make it home much more quickly. So grab a broom whenever you're ready; we've got work to do.

Leaders are–by definition–change makers. When you are called to lead, you are called to advance, move forward, and improve the situation.
–Anonymous

Rock Climbing

Sharp End of the Rope

In life, failures are inevitable. That means that everyone fails at something sometime. I don't say this to discourage you from doing anything but rather to encourage you to push through your failures. I was recently listening to a podcast featuring Gary Erickson, founder and co-owner of CLIF Bar and Company. His company makes energy bars for athletes on the go. During this podcast Erickson explained that while his company was still growing, it went through many rocky points. Early on he was sued by a rival company, then he almost lost the company to a distributor that also sued him. Later he had to raise more than $60 million to buy out his partner! With all of these things going on, Erickson hared that the only way he pushed through these setbacks was by remembering the sharp end of the rope.

Although Erickson was a founder and owner of a company, he was also an athlete who loved rock climbing. The expression *sharp end of the rope* is used in rock climbing to describe the leader in a two-person climb. In rock climbing, you're either leading or following. When two or more people are climbing together, they are connected by a system of ropes. If you're following, you're known as the second. In this position, if you take a misstep, your fall won't be far, because the leader is above you keeping the rope taut, or stretched out to its fullest. However, when you're leading, you're on the sharp end of the rope, because if you take a misstep, no one is above you to keep the rope taut. That means that if you fall, you have to fall past your second for the rope to become taut again. Erickson stated that while it is scary being in the lead, he eventually got used to facing danger and staying composed. Being in the lead made him focus more.

This is exactly the lesson that Jesus taught to Peter. In Matthew 26:34, in front of everyone, Jesus tells Peter that he will deny Him three times before the rooster crows. Peter must have felt embarrassed and even confused. Just a few chapters earlier, in Matthew 16, Jesus had commended Peter for understanding that Jesus was the Son of God. Jesus didn't point out Peter's weakness to discourage him but rather to encourage him through his inevitable failures. Jesus wanted Peter to focus.

Failures can act as distractions. And when you're distracted, you're not focused. Leaders will face more failures than the average person. But because a leader is a leader, it's important that no matter what, they never lose their focus.

You can't fall if you don't climb. But there's no joy
in living your whole life on the ground.
—Anonymous

Skiing

Skiing Lessons

When I was in middle school, I was privileged to go skiing twice each year. The first time I went skiing, I had to learn how to ski. For those of you who haven't done this before, one of the first things you have to learn is how to wedge your skis. To wedge skis means to point both feet inward and make an A with the skis. Wedging helps you slow down if you feel that you're going too fast. That first time I learned more than wedging. I learned how to come to a complete stop; how to successfully get on and off a ski lift; and, most important, how to read the difficulty of the different slopes.

As I made sure to learn everything our instructor was trying to teach us, I noticed that several of my friends were goofing off and not paying attention. At the end of the lesson we all got a little mark on our jackets that signified that we had learned everything. I thought it was unfair that my friends who hadn't paid attention got the same reward that I got. I didn't complain about it, though. After all, the mark on our jackets wasn't going to protect us from the dangers of the slopes. One friend crashed into the side of the lodge because she didn't know how to slow down. Another fell off the ski lift because he didn't get on it properly. A couple of my friends embarked on double black diamond slopes—not for beginners—and completely wiped out. After seeing the injuries pile up, I was thankful that I'd learned how to ski the right way.

In Habakkuk 1, the prophet questions God about all the unrighteous people who seem to prosper. You know, they're the people who cut in line during lunch, talk in class, gossip, or even cheat on their homework—and rarely get caught. Habakkuk asked God why He allows the cheaters of this world to not be punished.

The prophet was asking a very old question: Why do bad things happen to good people and the other way around? The answer to this can get really deep and philosophical, but what we should concentrate on is serving God, even if it seems that when we do the right thing it doesn't pay off. God will work everything out. I thought the cheaters in my ski lesson were getting away with it, but they ended up paying for it with the injuries they got. Things will happen in life no matter who you are. Just keep serving God, and He will take care of you.

He causes His sun to rise on the evil and the good, and sends rain on the righteous and the unrighteous.

"He causes His sun to rise on the evil and the good, and sends rain on the righteous and the unrighteous.
—Matthew 5:45, NASB

Hockey

Making the Save

Before every game, legendary National Hockey League (NHL) goaltender (informally called goalie) Henrik Lundqvist finds a quiet place free from distractions to clear his mind. When he finds this quiet place, he stretches. He does all types of stretches. They say he stretches before the game, during the game, and even after the game. The reason for the stretching? NHL goalies know that they have to be able to contort their bodies to make a save at a moment's notice. It's this practice that has propelled Lundquist to be one of the greatest goalies in NHL history.

Being a goalie is one of the most important jobs in the game of hockey and one of the most difficult in sports in general. Every game, goalies stand by themselves between two metal poles, guarding a net from puck shots from the opposing team. And the pucks aren't slow either. That small black piece of hard rubber can fly more than one hundred miles per hour! There are about thirty shots on goal per game and eighty-two games in each regular season, and although a goalie does not usually play every game, some goalies have seen more than two thousand shots in a season.

A good goalie is expected to save more than 90 percent. That means that if they let three goals or more past them per game, it's considered a failure. Although that is a tough margin of error, it's necessary because the success of the team depends on how well they can defend against attacks from opposing teams.

During the regular season the games are tough. But if a team makes it to the playoffs, everything intensifies. With each round of the playoffs, the stakes get higher as they get closer to winning a championship. That's why, to prepare for these moments, goalies such as Lundqvist find peace in doing their routine. They need to be completely focused on what is going on with the puck and what play may turn into a shot at a moment's notice.

As tough as it is to be an NHL goalie, you've been drafted to take on an even tougher assignment: guarding your heart. In Proverbs 4:23, the Bible tells us: "Above all else, guard your heart, for everything you do flows from it" (NIV). Every day we face shots from the enemy, who is trying to score every chance he gets. As the Bible rightly states, everything that we do comes from what's inside our hearts. Just as Henry Lundqvist finds a quiet place before each game to prepare his body for all sorts of attacks, we need to do the same with our hearts. Don't let anything distract you. Spend time talking to God every day, and He will help you make saves at more than 90 percent.

Guard your time fiercely. Be generous with it, but be intentional about it.
—David duChemin

God Loves It When You Help Him Spread His Word

In most sports, the only person credited with an assist is the player who directly helps another player score. In hockey, however, more than one player can be credited with an assist. In other words, if player A passes the puck to player B, then player B passes the puck to player C, and then player C scores, players A and B both receive credit for an assist.

One day I read Psalm 118:22, which says, "The stone the builders rejected has become the cornerstone" (NIV). I like this verse a lot, because it reminds me of the "redemption" of a player, someone who others didn't think was very good but later proved them wrong.

Strangely enough, later that same day I was at a girls' volleyball practice. One of the players was feeling down because she wasn't a starter yet. I remembered the Psalm I had read earlier. I passed this message on to the player and she ended up having a much better practice and felt better about herself.

The next year, that player became a starter and a key piece to the team's success. I was happy that I was able to use something I had read in the Bible to help someone have a better outlook.

Whenever I read anything in the Bible and I'm able to share it, I like to think of it as a hockey assist. When God shows me something I can use to help people understand the Bible more, and people take that and grow from it, it's another "assist" for me.

Imagine that biblical truths are like a hockey puck, which is actually quite small. We pass that hockey puck to others so they can score the ultimate goal of being with Jesus forever. That's a big deal!

Don't you want to pass it on?

You'll never catch me bragging about goals,
but I'll talk all you want about my assists.
—Wayne Gretzky

Golf

The Follow-Through

People say that golf is a game of precision. A good golfer can consistently place the ball in a good position on the fairway, but that depends on a golfer's swing.

A good swing can make the person look like a legend. A bad swing will make the person look far worse than a novice. If you want to see an example of a bad swing, do a search for "Charles Barkley golf swing" on Google and get ready for laughs.

Anyone who wants to pick up golf as a sport can get frustrated. Golfers may be tempted to ignore technique and just try to power the ball down the fairway. This means that they may try to swing really hard at the ball, but if they do that, success can vary. The golfer will likely hit the ball in the wrong direction or miss the ball completely!

Golf is less about brute strength and more about physics. For those of you who like science and math, you may be able to break down a good golf swing versus a bad one. As I watched numerous clips of such golf greats as Jack Nicklaus, Tiger Woods, and Arnold Palmer, I noticed that all of them have a great follow-through. A follow-through is the part of the golf swing after the golfer hits the ball. They hold this picturesque pose for about three seconds as they watch the ball sail down the fairway. Ultimately the follow-through helps guide the ball farther in the direction you want it to go.

Following through in real life means to finish a task completely. For example, if you were assigned to do your homework, but you did only half the problem, then you didn't follow through. Get it?

Jesus wants us to have follow-through as witnesses for Him. He wants us to do everything He asks us to do with a willing and cheerful heart. If you have accepted the call to be a witness for Jesus, then make sure you have great follow-through!

In golf as in life it is the follow-through that makes the difference.
—Anonymous

Extreme Sports

How Tough Are You?

What if I told you that today you are going to receive electric shocks and get muddy, cold, and possibly bloody? Do you think this would be fun? If you said yes, then you would probably like to join the more than 1.3 million people who have participated in a Tough Mudder event.

A Tough Mudder is designed to test physical strength and mental toughness along a ten- to twelve-mile obstacle course. In this team-oriented event, friendship is more important than finishing the race ahead of everyone else. It's not a timed race, but rather a team challenge that allows everyone involved to experience exhilarating, safe, world-class obstacles.

In a Tough Mudder, the goal is simply to finish. There's one obstacle called Electroshock Therapy. To complete this section, participants must run through dangling live wires that, if touched, result in a painful shock. There's another challenge called King of the Mountain, in which everyone has to climb a sixteen-foot wall of hay. There are several other obstacles that can be overcome only with the help of someone else.

In some ways, the Christian journey is very much like the Tough Mudder. Our ultimate goal is to make it to heaven, but there will be many obstacles that stand in our way.

For example, on the road to heaven you will face tough choices that separate you from those who aren't concerned with pleasing Jesus. These decisions start off very small, such as resisting the urge to steal candy—but then eventually grow to become bigger decisions, such as whether to pay tithe.

Sometimes these decisions are too much for us to handle on our own. So to help us with these decisions, or challenges, we have friends. The best Friend we can call on is Jesus. By the help that we give one another, we develop an unbreakable bond of friendship.

Don't you want to share heaven, especially Jesus, with your friends? Whether it's a Tough Mudder, making it to heaven, or any personal goals you may have, there will always be obstacles in your way. Your friends and Jesus will be there to help carry you through.

The idea of Tough Mudder is not really to win, but . . . to have a story to tell.
—John Branch

Skateboarding

My Hero, the Hawk

When I was in middle school, I paid attention to only two sports: basketball and soccer. That was it. After living in Minnesota for a couple of years, I discovered this cool sport called skateboarding. Guys in my school were always jumping on parts of the jungle gym with their Soap shoes and pretending to be skateboarders.

Just like I tried to imitate Michael Jordan on the court, the cool kids wore Soap shoes to imitate Tony Hawk. I had no idea who he was until I saw him on TV.

Wow! Hawk made skateboarding cool for everyone. I was in awe every time I saw him on a skateboard. He made even the simplest tricks look amazing. You could say that Hawk kick-flipped his way into my heart.

One day at a skateboarding competition, Hawk was the first person to land the 900, a trick that involves spinning around on your skateboard two and a half times. Only nine people in the world have officially done this trick.

Suddenly there were Hawk video games, shoes, skateboards, and even movies. He was immortalized in sports history with that trick. After that, everyone and their mother wanted to skateboard—all because of Tony Hawk!

When I read the Bible, I am amazed at how many lives Jesus touched or changed. I'm not saying Hawk is like Jesus, but I do believe one person can make a big difference.

Think about it: through the woman at the well, Bartimaeus the blind beggar, and even the centurion's servant, Jesus influenced people to follow Him. All it took was one positive interaction with Jesus.

Hawk will never know how many people love skateboarding because of him (just like I'll never know how many of you actually read this book). The important thing is that we all try our best to be witnesses for what we believe in. The way you act could influence the next great leader. First John 3:18 says: "Dear children, let us not love with words or speech but with actions and in truth" (NIV).

Hawk made skateboarding cool, and many skateboarders say he is the reason they started skateboarding. If Tony Hawk can influence people to skateboard, what can you do to influence people to follow Jesus?

I consider skateboarding an art form, a lifestyle, and a sport.
—Tony Hawk

Racquetball

A Matter of Obedience

One afternoon my brother asked me if I wanted to play racquetball. I didn't know the rules, but after a short instructional speech, I quickly grasped the concept. The one thing I did know about racquetball was that people who played the sport always wore protective eyewear. I didn't bother asking my brother about this, since we were just playing for fun. He was going to take it easy on me. We played for about two hours. I had a blast—even though I lost every game!

That evening I went home and searched YouTube for videos showing how to improve at racquetball. All the videos I watched said players must wear protective eyewear. Again, I ignored these warnings since I had already played for two hours and hadn't walked away looking like a Cyclops.

The next day I played with my brother again. We'd been playing for about thirty minutes when the inevitable happened. I served the ball against the wall and watched as it bounced back over my head. I followed the ball, and it landed squarely in front of my brother, who was perfectly positioned to return the serve. I watched in slow motion as he arched his arm backward. That's when I realized I was right in front of where he wanted to hit the ball. As fast as my brain works, it wasn't fast enough to get out of the way. My brother had swung his arm forward at full power, and the next thing I saw was the blue racquetball about five feet in front of my face. I barely had time to close my eyes before I felt the sharp sting of the ball slam against my left eye. I immediately doubled over in pain from my eye. It felt like a million little people were jumping up and down on top of it. Thankfully there was no blood, and I was fine. My cornea was a little sore for several days, but at least I still had my eye.

When I was bent over in pain, I remember thinking, *This is why you're supposed to wear protective eyewear.* Then I thought about all the warnings I'd ignored and how lucky I'd been not to get seriously injured.

Disobedience has its price. We've all done things that we know we shouldn't have. Sometimes we get punished, and sometimes we don't, but there are always consequences for our actions. I thought that the rules of racquetball didn't apply to me, because I wasn't immediately "punished" for not wearing protective eyewear. However, the consequences caught up to me later. Learn from my mistakes. Learn from your mistakes. It's better to obey than to disobey.

Obedience is an act of faith; disobedience is the result of unbelief.
–Edwin Louis Cole

Olympics

Be Brave

In 1968, Eunice Kennedy Shriver stood in front of the audience at the inaugural Special Olympics. What had started off as a day camp for children with intellectual disabilities in her Potomac, Maryland, home had blossomed into the Special Olympics. Eunice was part of the famous Kennedy family; her brother was President John F. Kennedy. Eunice started Camp Shriver to give children with mental disabilities a place to play. She grew concerned for the mentally disabled partly because of her sister Rosemary, who had a mental disability.

When she stood in front of that first crowd, Kennedy wanted to inspire them. She cleared her throat and said, "In ancient Rome the gladiators went into the arena with these words on their lips: let me win, but if I cannot win, let me be brave in the attempt." Those words turned into the Special Olympics motto and are repeated by the athletes in the games to this day.

That thought resonated with a lot of people, and the Special Olympics grew into a huge event. Today more than 5.3 million athletes from 170 different countries participate in the games.

Being brave in the attempt is crucial. The fear of losing can keep you from succeeding.

There was a woman in the Bible who had to be very brave. Her uncle Mordecai told her that she would have to go in front of the king to tell him about an evil plot against her people. The catch? She had to do that without the king's invitation. Back in her day, people went before the king only with an invitation. If the king was displeased with a person's uninvited presence, the penalty was death! This woman needed to be brave to take on such a task. But after much prayerful consideration, Esther came to a decision: she would go to see the king. She was willing to risk her life if there was a chance that she could save her people.

As she walked toward the king, her heart trembled. But with an inner peace, she made her approach. The king accepted her into his court without an invitation, and Esther went on to become a great queen for her people. You can read about it in the book of Esther.

The Bible tells us that we have nothing to fear. We must always approach every situation expecting the best outcome. And if we don't at first achieve success, we simply dust ourselves off and try again.

To uncover your true potential, you must first find your own limits, and then you have to have the courage to blow past them!
—Picabo Street

All for One, One for All

Most sports that are played usually involve some teamwork, but bobsledding, NASCAR pit crews, and relay races rely heavily on teamwork. If one person fails, the whole team fails.

During the 2008 Beijing Olympics the American men's and women's relay teams both made a huge mistake. In a relay race, the most important thing to remember is not to drop the baton. When the women's team started their race, everything was going well. The baton was perfectly passed during the first three legs, but then on the final leg Torri Edwards mishandled the pass to Lauryn Williams. As the baton dropped to the ground, Edwards held her hands over her face, horrified that she had made such a costly mistake.

Later, in the men's race, the American team faced a similar situation. Just as in the women's race, the first three legs went perfectly; however, on the handoff, Darvis Patton accidentally placed the baton in the wrong spot for Tyson Gay. Above the groans of the crowd, the metallic ping of the baton bouncing around on the track was probably the only thing those two runners heard.

In the time between Olympics, athletes train really hard to make sure they're ready, because if they make a mistake, they have to wait another four years before they can try again. The sad part about relay races and other team sports is that even if the other team members don't mess up, they have to be identified with the failure of the one person who makes the mistake.

From the Bible we understand that sin entered the world because of the mistake of Adam. However, in Romans 5:12–19, Paul has a wonderful thought and tells us that even though one person made a mistake, and all suffered because of it, Jesus came down and died for us so that we could all win. Isn't that a cool parallel? One person made a mistake, and we all had to suffer. So in turn one righteous Person had to die to save us all.

The mistake in each of the relay races was made by one person, but often, mistakes in sports can't be undone by one person. Athletes usually have to wait for another chance at redemption. That's just the nature of sports. Thankfully, we don't have to wait for our redemption. God has already given it to us through one Man: Jesus. Although all were condemned to death because of one, it was One who took the punishment for us all.

A team will always appreciate a great individual
if he's willing to sacrifice for the group.
—Kareem Abdul-Jabbar

Rowing

Someone's Looking Out for You

I love canoeing. There's something about the mystique of it all. I remember being at North Star Camp in Brainerd, Minnesota. I would untether the canoe and push out onto the Mississippi River. At that point it was just nature and me. For better or for worse, I was in control of how fast or slow I went. I loved it. Occasionally my friends and I would race canoes, and we had a lot of fun.

It wasn't until much later in life that I learned about a sport that reminds me of canoeing. Rowing is the official title of the sport, and it comes in many different forms. For example, there's the eight-person rowing team, or simply "eights." The crazy thing about eights is that unlike canoeing, the rowers must have their backs facing their destination. That's because it's much faster to row backward than to paddle forward.

For those who can't get a mental picture, imagine that the driver's seat in a car is turned around so that the driver can look out the rear window only. Insane, right? Thankfully, there's a solution for eights: a person called the coxswain, or cox for short. The cox has three main goals:

1. Keep the boat and rowers safe.
2. Be in command of the boat at all times.
3. Provide motivation and encouragement to the crew.

The cox has to steer the boat, because obviously the rowers can't see where they're going. The cox has to tell them how hard to row, when to slow down or speed up, and so on. One of the things I find cool is the last goal: to motivate and encourage the crew. The rowers don't know how close they are to their destination, so it's up to the cox to let them know. The cox is there to push them physically and mentally. When the rowers are at their weakest, the cox steps in to tell them to keep going.

I like to think of myself as a rower. In fact, all Christians are rowers. Often when things don't work out for us, we become discouraged and depressed. That's when God steps in as our coxswain. We don't know where we're going in this life, so it's up to God to steer us in the right direction. And when we're at our lowest point, He's there to keep us going, to motivate and encourage us. The important thing to remember is that no matter what, God is in control of our boats at all times.

Rowing, like success, is a journey, not a destination.
–Rick Clother

Our Strengths for Others' Weaknesses

It was the Olympics rowing final in one small part of the world on August 22, 2004. Sally Robbins, a member of the Australian rowing team, had trained for this moment and was ready to help her team win. When the race started, team Australia held a good position for the first thousand meters. However, with five hundred meters remaining, they were in fifth place. That's when things got worse. With only four hundred meters left in the race,

Robbins purposely dropped her oar in the water and stopped rowing. Even though other members of her team kept rowing, the Australian team came in dead last.

Robbins had a meltdown on one of the world's biggest stages, and this wasn't the first time. In 2002, at the World Rowing Championships, Australia was rowing well and maintaining first place. But again, with four hundred meters left in the race, Robbins stopped rowing. Team Australia slipped from first place and finished in fourth place. Both times, her teammates were devastated and angry. One newspaper covering the event wrote, "In a team sport such as rowing, what she did was unforgivable. It appears Robbins committed the greatest crime there is in honest sport: she quit."*

When asked about it, Robbins responded by saying that she had pushed herself too hard. She hadn't quit; her body had been exhausted to the point that she had collapsed. Whether anyone believes her doesn't really matter. What happened, happened. However, the saddest part of Robbin's story is that she didn't get enough support from her teammates to keep rowing when she felt weak.

There was a time in the Bible when Moses felt weak as well, but his ending turned out much differently (see Exodus 17:8–16). Moses and the Israelites were in battle against the Amalekites. While the army was fighting, Moses was on top of a hill watching it all. As as long as he held up the staff of God in his hands, the Israelites would win, but whenever he dropped his hands, the Amalekites would win. Seeing this, Aaron and Hur, two of Moses' teammates, told Moses to sit down while they held his arms up for the entire battle. They did this until sunset, and eventually the Israelites won.

Unlike Robbin's situation, when Moses grew tired, his

* "Robbins Drops Oar, Team Drops Bundle," *The Sydney Morning Herald*, August 24, 2004, 8:40, https://www.smh.com.au/sport/robbins-drops-oar-team-drops-bundle-20040824-gdjlyw.html.

teammates were able to help him to victory. One of the best things about team sports is actual teamwork. Working together with others, under any condition, forces us to pay attention to one another so we can cover their weaknesses with our strengths and vice versa. Let the story of Sally Robbins serve as a reminder–not of what failure looks like but rather of the opportunities we have in which we can help others succeed.

You don't inspire your teammates by showing them how amazing you are. You inspire them by showing them how amazing they are.
–Robyn Benincasa

Coaching

Angry Love

Has your coach ever yelled at you? Mine did once. The score was close at halftime, but our basketball team wasn't playing well. We should've easily been winning. Our coach was angry and raised his voice as he pointed out all the things that we were doing wrong.

My first reaction was to get mad at our coach, but then I realized that he wasn't really angry; he was frustrated that our team wasn't executing the way we'd been trained. Our coach loved us, and he knew that we could do better.

As any coach will tell you, it's super frustrating to tell players to do something and then watch them not follow through on your instructions. During the years that I have been a coach, I've watched dozens of players ignore my instructions. I don't take it personally, but it is very frustrating to be ignored. I don't believe in yelling at players to correct their behavior, but when I see coaches do it, I understand the place that it comes from.

Think about the first time you read the story of Jesus cleansing the temple. When Jesus saw the vendors disrespecting God's house by selling in the temple, He became angry. The Bible says that Jesus used a whip to drive the merchants out of the temple. "He overturned the tables of the money changers and the benches of those selling doves. 'It is written,' he said to them, ' "My house will be called a house of prayer," but you are making it "a den of robbers" ' " (Matthew 21:12, 13, NIV). This is one of the few times where Jesus chose to express His disappointment with fury. He wasn't angry at the people but their actions. It's a bit like when your parents discipline you and tell you that it will hurt them more than it will hurt you. I'm sure it hurt Jesus to take that kind of action, but it was necessary discipline.

We may think of Jesus as our heavenly coach. Similar to a sports coach, He's given us instructions on how to win at the game of life. When we don't follow His instructions, such as loving God with all our hearts and our neighbor as ourselves (see Matthew 22:37–39), He must be incredibly disappointed and frustrated. Knowing what it's like to disappoint a human coach makes me even more careful to try to not disappoint God.

A word of encouragement during a failure is worth more than an hour of praise after success.
—Anonymous

A Page From My Secret Journal

On August 9, 2012, I became an academy athletic director. I can't tell you how excited I am at the opportunity to do this job! The position involves managing all the school's sports teams. More important to me, though, is that my new position allows me to be involved in ministry. It's now my job to combine sports and Christianity for students to show them that they have a chance to witness every time they play.

You may have met some people who don't believe that sports should be mixed with Christianity. Often those same people believe that competition corrupts. I don't necessarily agree with that. Sure, competition does sometimes bring out the worst in people. But I think competition can be a good thing, because it teaches players what it's like to be a winner and also what it's like to lose.

So what does the Bible say about competition? The best answer comes from the apostle Paul in 1 Corinthians 9:25, "Everyone who competes in the games goes into strict training. They do it to get a crown that will not last, but we do it to get a crown that will last forever" (NIV).

One thing I see in this Bible passage is that when non-Christians play sports, they do it for the earthly glory it brings. The trophies, the money, and the attention are all earthly treasures. But people who are serious about following Jesus are going after something more important: an everlasting prize.

When Christians play sports, our goal should still be to win, but our efforts should always reflect a Christlike attitude. Through the games we play, we can be a witness to others that might not know about God. The main thing we need to keep in mind is that sports should never replace God. Ellen G. White even warned her students in Battle Creek about this:

"The place that should have been occupied by Jesus was [replaced] by your passion for games. You chose your amusements instead of the comfort of the Holy Spirit."*

Like anything done in excess, obsessing over sports is unhealthy. God wants us to be healthy and happy. If playing sports makes you happy, great! Just don't let sports replace God. Keep Him first, and He'll direct your path. Love God. Like sports. That's the motto.

We shouldn't give up activities that provide exercise and recreation. However, these activities should be kept strictly within bounds so that they do not lose their purpose and feed the desire for self-centeredness.

—Adapted from Ellen G. White, *Manuscript Releases*, vol. 1, 391

---

* Ellen G. White, *Selected Messages*, book 1 (Hagerstown, MD: Review and Herald®, 1958), 136, italics added.

Diving

Cage the Fear

Fear is a wild thing. It's an emotion that causes three responses: confront, run, or freeze. Fear can control people and affect the way they live. These days I'm fine, but there was a time that fear had control over me.

I'll never forget the first time I dived into a pool. I was in fourth grade, and it was the final test of my swimming class. All students were required to dive headfirst into the deep end of the pool, which to me seemed about twenty feet deep.

My swim instructor made each of the students go one by one. I quickly excused myself and hid in the bathroom. It was about five minutes before someone was sent in to get me. My feet felt like lead as I plodded out to the pool. All eyes were on me, and I was terrified. I started crying even before I got to the edge of the pool. It was messy, as in runny-nose, blubbering-little-boy messy. Even with the tears pouring down my cheeks and snot running out of my nose, my instructor showed no mercy. He kept coaxing me to dive. I was fine when I was swimming close to the edge, but now I was forced to dive into the middle of the deep end. This was scary! I had never done this before. Why did my instructor want me to do something I was so afraid to do?

After what seemed like hours, and with much encouragement, I finally dived. I remember the cold water hitting my fingertips and slowly engulfing the rest of my body. I thought, *Hey, that wasn't too bad!* I doggie-paddled back to the edge, and life continued as normal.

This year the gymnastics team at the school where I serve as athletic director has adopted the motto Cage the Fear. It's based on 2 Timothy 1:7, which says, "For the Spirit God gave us does not make us timid, but gives us power, love and self-discipline" (NIV). My swim instructor knew that I was ready to dive into the pool even if I didn't believe it myself. What I should've done was trust that my instructor knew what he was doing.

This is the same way our heavenly Father looks out for us. When I get scared or nervous, I just think back to that time at the pool. I know that God is in control and that all He wants me to do is dive. No matter how crazy the situation may seem, God is always in control. As part of God's family, we have nothing to fear. It's up to us to overcome our earthly fears so that God can use us in the way He needs. All you need to do is cage the fear.

Courage is resistance to fear, mastery of fear–not absence of fear.
–Mark Twain

Going for the Win

Franchise Players

Did you know that most sports teams have what are called *franchise* players? This title is reserved for players who are the "faces" of the team. They embody everything a particular team is about. In the NBA, Chris Paul was the Los Angeles Clippers' franchise player. He was a selfless player and actively looked to get his teammates involved. He was also a fierce competitor and competed with the best of the best in world competitions.

In the NFL, the Dallas Cowboys' franchise player was Tony Romo. In the NHL, the Pittsburgh Penguins got a franchise player when they signed Sidney Crosby.

Genuine franchise players tend to have one thing in common: the ability to lead.

If you are the owner of a franchise, you want your franchise player to be able to inspire others to acheive greatness. The franchise player should be able to extract the best from all the players around him or her. Unfortunately, there are times that a franchise player doesn't live up to their title. If they have a bad attitude or a terrible work ethic, it can be very harmful to a team. A helpful way to describe the effects of a bad franchise player is through a biology lesson I learned while watching a movie. Check it out:

"What happens to a stagnant cell?" the narrator asked. "A cell that is not in motion is not a productive member of the system. It ends up assuming all the other cells are going to pick up the slack somewhere, but they don't. They imitate the stray cell until basically the whole organism begins to die. . . .

"Here's the good news: All that decay can be restored. Once that cell is back on track, it creates energy amongst the other cells.. . . . It starts getting a little movement going. . . .And this is the beginning of the restorative process. . . . If all the cells work together, what will happen? The entire system is healed."*

Did any of you catch the similarities between the stagnant cell and a bad franchise player? If one cell stops working, the rest of the cells begin to imitate that behavior. Essentially, the habits that the franchise player displays is what everyone else will copy.

Jesus is our franchise player for Christianity. That's why it's so important that we imitate His life on earth as best as possible. Go out there and act like a franchise player for your school or family. If we all do it, then the entire system can be healed.

A leader is best when people barely know he exists. When his work is done, his aim fulfilled, they will say: "We did it ourselves."
–Lao Tzu

Women in Sports

On March 19, 1975, Pennsylvania became the first state that allowed girls to compete with boys in high school sports. It seems strange that it would take that long for something like that to happen. Somewhere along the line, our society incorrectly thought that women were inferior to men. Now, it's debatable which sports women are better at than men, but the big picture is that they

* "Science Lesson," *Here Comes the Boom*, directed by Frank Coraci (2012 Culver City, CA: Sony Picture Home Entertainment, 2013), DVD.

should have an equal opportunity to play.

It took a long time, by about 1973 to be exact, before women could participate in many professional leagues. For example, now we have women's basketball, soccer, and golf. With the invention of those leagues we also have some of the biggest names in sports belonging to women.

Venus and Serena Williams are two sisters that took the tennis world by storm with their athletic abilities. Danica Patrick broke the mold when she began racing in motor sports. And Brittney Griner wowed many when she took her six-foot-eight-inch frame and led her Baylor basketball team to an impressive record 40–0 season.

It's not unusual to see a woman on the headlines of ESPN, but in the past it wasn't easy for a woman athlete to be in the news. However, one of the first turning points in women's history in sports was a tennis match between Billie Jean King and Bobby Riggs. In a nationally televised event, King played and beat Riggs in what was called the Battle of the Sexes. The ripple effect from this game allowed for even more women to compete in sports.

The first four books of the New Testament are written for different audiences. The story of Jesus that Matthew tells seems well suited to clarify the identity, vocation, and practices of a community in transition and distress. Some people believe the book of Luke highlights Jesus showing how important women are to ministry.

The men in Bible times felt that women didn't belong in important places where decisions were being made. Jesus gave people a different perspective on the value of women in ministry. From the woman at the well to Mary Magdalene, Jesus always had the utmost respect for women and treated them as equals. If Jesus treats women that way, shouldn't we?

The way some women are portrayed in our society nowadays isn't always positive. TV shows, movies, and music that you listen to often degrade what being a woman really means. Do me and Jesus a favor by taking the time to give all the women you know a big pat on the back for all the positive things they have done and continue to do. Trust me, they'll love it!

Keep your dreams alive. Understand that to achieve anything requires faith and belief in yourself, vision, hard work, determination, and dedication.
—Gail Devers

After the Win

How many of you have ever played king of the hill? It's a rough game, I know, but it's so much fun! I remember playfully tossing my challengers aside as I fought to remain king for as long as possible. Sadly, someone always dethroned me and I had to start over. Eventually I would become too tired to climb the mountain and I'd stop playing.

Did you know that professional athletes play king of the hill too? It's a different version of the game, but think about it. Every year our favorite teams strive to be national champions. We watch as athletes make amazing shots, spectacular catches, and unbelievable saves—all for the right to declare themselves champions. People such as Wayne Gretzky, Michael Jordan, Edson "Pelé" Arantes do Nascimento, and Joe Montana have all climbed the "hill" many times, but where are they now? Well, age-wise they're all "over the hill" and no one really pays much attention to them anymore!

Sure, broadcasters have given them credit and praise for what they did in their primes, but we all know they can't play at their previous level anymore. So what do we do as fans? We watch and wait for the next superstar.

Have you ever thought about what will happen after you're done playing sports for your school or team? Some of you may go on to play professionally, but the majority of you will move on to concentrate on college, studies, and blah, blah, blah. All your fans will miss you, but the sport doesn't stop—it keeps going.

Earthly glory is fleeting, which means it passes very quickly. All the championships in the world can't stop old age or broken bones. In fact, there was a person in the Bible who also had a brush with fame: King Saul.

Saul had it all: height, good looks, and a muscular build. It was obvious why the people accepted Saul as their king. As he became comfortable in his new leadership role, he also became accustomed to praise. Saul started falling in love with the idea that he was actually responsible for Israel's victories. He slowly began forgetting that God had placed him in his current position. One day after a battle against the Amalekites, Saul disobeyed God's rules, and it cost him dearly. Because of his disobedience and his love of self-glory, God could not continue to bless Saul and allow him to lead His people. From that moment on, Saul's life took a downward spiral as he desperately tried to gain back God's favor. You can read about it in 1 Samuel 15.

The same thing holds true in sports. I love sports as much as the next person (maybe more), but if earthly treasures such as championships and MVP trophies distract us, then we lose sight of our real purpose. Now I'm not saying winning is bad—I always play to win! Just know that our ultimate goal is to be a witness first and a winner second.

Talent is God-given. Be humble. Fame is man-given.
Be grateful. Conceit is self-given. Be careful.
—John Wooden

Don't Lose the Ultimate Game

I've probably seen a million game-winning moments. I've seen Robert Horry's buzzer-beater in 2002 against the Kings. I've seen Doug Flutie's Hail Mary football pass and, more recently, Maya Moore leading her Huskies to an NCAA championship and a current win streak of 78–0!

But one thing I don't get to see often is the story about the losing team. I don't think there are too many documentaries on a team losing the big game.

Losing is one of the hardest things to deal with. I've been on the losing side of a big game before, and it stinks. While the other team is parading around, you're stuck there feeling empty, confused, and stunned. The normal reaction is to cry or walk away in anger. I think it's safe to say that no one likes to lose.

During the "madness" of March 2010, there was a women's Elite Eight game between Xavier and Stanford. The game was tied at fifty-three with sixteen seconds left in the game. Xavier's senior Dee Dee Jernigan missed not one but two uncontested lay-ups in a row! Stanford recovered the ball with four seconds left and called a time-out.

Jernigan immediately squatted down, buried her face in her hands, and wept. Not like, "Oh, she's crying because I can see a tear streaming down her face," but actual weeping. It was so heartbreaking that the coach had to walk out onto the floor and physically pick her up to get her back to the bench.

Inconsolable is the word that ESPN's Stuart Scott used to describe her. It was truly a sad moment.

So what do you say in moments like that? Anyone who has ever been in that position knows that there is nothing to say. No number of words can comfort you. To fail or come up short in a big moment is devastating.

Psalm 34:18 tells us that Jesus is always with the brokenhearted and those who are crushed in spirit. King David must have felt emotionally drained when he wrote this. Saul was chasing him through every nook and cranny in Israel, even though David had done nothing wrong. David had tried his hardest to be nice to Saul, but to no avail. Saul's jealousy was far too great.

I've heard critics say that big games define people. However, I like to think that what you do after a big game is what defines you. Meaning it doesn't matter what you accomplished in the game, win or lose, but rather how you let it affect you. Sometimes people don't perform well in big games, but that doesn't mean they're losers. But if after a big loss you wander aimlessly through life always thinking back to how you messed up, then you have lost at an even bigger game: the game of life.

The price of success is hard work, dedication to the job at hand,
and the determination that whether we win or lose,
we have applied the best of ourselves to the task at hand.
—Vince Lombardi

The Amazing Water-Powered Body

There he was, tied up and surrounded by a thousand men who wanted him dead. At a glance the competition appeared to be stacked against him, but he had a secret weapon. Samson had the Lord on his team.

In Judges 15:13, Samson's future seemed bleak. But whenever the Spirit of the Lord came on Samson, no one could stop him. Samson looked around, found a jawbone of a donkey, and, well, made the opposition an offer they couldn't refuse.

Now here's the interesting thing. In verse 18, the Bible says that he was thirsty. I wasn't around back then, but after disposing of a thousand men, I'm sure I would be dehydrated too. (Can you even count to a thousand without drinking something?) Samson cried out to God that he was going to die of thirst, so God opened up a place in the earth, and water came out of it. The Bible says: "When Samson drank, his strength returned and he revived" (verse 19, NIV). Samson definitely missed out on some sports drink business deals, but he nailed the hydration part.

Samson knew he needed water. Have you ever felt that urge in the middle of a game? During a time-out you'll see players guzzling down fresh, cool water. You can't go for too long without liquids. Coaches and players around the world will tell you that. I mean, look at all the commercials for Gatorade!

Unfortunately for some players, professional and amateur, getting dehydrated has had fatal consequences. The list is too long to put here, but you can look it up on the internet.

It's important that we replenish our electrolytes so that we don't suddenly collapse during a game, but what about in our spiritual lives? Are you getting your sips of the Bible during your day? I'm not talking about worship in the classroom or with your parents; I'm talking about your personal time with God. If the only worship you get is in a classroom, that's like saying you drink water only in the shower.

Just as you need to drink water, you need to read your Bible. Reading and studying your Bible replenishes your spiritual side. It helps keep you fresh so that you can face all the challenges you come across in life. So remember to drink not only water for your body, but also water for your soul.
—Leslie Bonci

The Roaring Crowd

If you know anything about the Colosseum in ancient Rome, you know that the gladiators fought for the approval of the crowd. Caesar's thumbs-up or thumbs-down rating, which meant life or death for the gladiator, depended mostly on what the crowd wanted to happen.

Nowadays the outcome of a sports event isn't decided by the crowd, but the spectators are still an undeniable factor. The NBA's Utah Jazz are nearly unbeatable at home in part because of the energy and noise of the home crowd. In a survey, NBA players ranked the Jazz's gym as the toughest to play in.* Some other intimidating arenas are Heinz Field, where the Terrible Towels wave

---

* Andrew Macaluso, "NBA's Five Toughest Places to Play," Dime Magazine, UPROXX, October 6, 2010, https://uproxx.com/dimemag/nbas-5-toughest-places-to-play/.

for the Pittsburgh Steelers and the Cameron Indoor Arena, home of the Duke Blue Devils basketball team, where Coach K and his Crazies reside.

"There's plenty of research out there which says crowds have an effect on athlete performance," says Matt Jevon, a sports psychologist.

The sportswriter used the phrase "psychologically frail" to describe opposing players who cannot block out the noise of the crowd. Ultimately these players don't perform well in such distracting situations.

"You can't be human and not notice these things," says Jevon. "The more you try and block something out the more you have to deal with it."*

So crowds do have an effect on some opposing players, but what about the home team? Some lab studies show that along with being a motivational tool, the crowd can also have a negative effect. It's as if players are too nervous to play well because they don't want to disappoint the crowd in a big moment.

Well, if "psychologically frail" were a club, then Pilate would definitely be one of its founders. During Jesus' trials Pilate had his opportunity to let his home crowd affect him negatively or positively. Unfortunately, he was too nervous to perform well. Matthew 27:18 says that Pilate "knew it was out of self-interest that they had handed Jesus over to him" (NIV)—meaning he knew Jesus was innocent. Pilate tried to get the crowd to free Jesus with the Barabbas option, but like spoiled children the stubborn spectators started to throw a tantrum. When Pilate saw that the crowd was getting angry, he washed his hands of Jesus and handed Him over.

What a coward. Instead of going with what he knew was right, Pilate decided to please the crowd. It sounds a lot like peer pressure, doesn't it? Like the crowds in sports stadiums, peer pressure

---

* "Does the Crowd Affect the Result," *BBC News Magazine*, July 1, 2008, 13:51, http://news.bbc.co.uk/2/hi/uk_news/magazine/7482972.stm.

can affect you in good or bad ways. Are you going to let the crowd affect your decisions, or are you going to affect the crowd? The answer is often the difference between a leader and a follower.

A tough day at the office is even tougher when your office contains spectator seating.
–Nik Posa

The Essential Time-Out

Whenever a game begins getting out of hand, the first thing a coach will do is call a time-out. All of the players will huddle by their team's bench while the coach tries to refocus the team. A time-out lets players take a quick vacation from the game. They use that time to think about what they need to do. Taking time-outs can help players get a fresh angle on an old situation. Sometimes they use it just to catch their breath. Then they can reenter the game fresh and ready to play.

People often compare life itself to a game. We chalk up wins and losses in our lives just like a team. Just as teams need time-outs, so do we. Every once in a while it's good to step away from sports. You have to call your own time-out.

Sometimes we can become so involved in sports that it's all we think about. For me, I used to play, think, and breathe basketball. It was my life. If I wasn't playing basketball, I was watching or thinking about it. Basketball consumed me. Do you know anyone like that?

What eventually happened was that my life became unbalanced. My life was too centered on basketball, and that's not good. There needs to be a proper balance in everything in your life. Otherwise you can't mature properly.

I needed a time-out. I needed a break from everything concerning basketball so I could develop or strengthen other sides of my life, such as my writing.

Every so often Jesus would take a time-out too. He would

leave the crowds and even His disciples to find a quiet place where He could think about what He needed to do. Whether it was a short time-out, such as in the Garden of Gethsemane, or a long one, such as His forty days and nights in the wilderness, Jesus regularly took time-outs. He used that time to refocus on His task at hand. He also would receive instructions and guidance from His "coach": God.

Doing anything for a long period of time gets boring. If you haven't done so already, take a time-out. Instead of playing sports, use the time to do something else. Read a book. Take a nature walk. Do a crossword puzzle. Just do something to take your mind off sports. By doing this, you'll be refreshed to take on your specific sport with new energy.

If it hadn't been for my time-out, I probably wouldn't have this column to share with you. Just imagine what you could accomplish with your time-out!

Rest when you're weary. Refresh and renew yourself, your body, your mind, your spirit. Then get back to work.
—Ralph Marston

The Outsiders

Athletes are admired by many people around the world. However, the admiration doesn't stop at the professional level. No, no, no—it even trickles right down to your school. Think about it: How are student athletes viewed in your school? Are they ignored? Do people generally dislike them and throw rotten food at them? Of course not. Student athletes are often greatly admired, and if you're one of them, you know the feeling.

From one (former) student athlete to another, what do you do with all this attention? I once read (OK, in a Spider-Man comic) that great power comes with great responsibility, but what does that mean?

Well, I found a good example in the Bible. Even though Jesus wasn't known as an athlete, He still was considered a superstar. Jesus rarely got a moment by Himself, because He was constantly surrounded by crowds of people. It was almost as if Jesus were on a world tour or something.

One time in particular (Luke 19:1–10) Jesus was walking through Jericho, and then all of a sudden He stopped. It was almost as if He were looking for someone. Ah! There! Up in the . . . tree? Yup. Zacchaeus was perched on one of the highest branches of a sycamore tree just to catch a glimpse of Jesus. Even back then people were doing crazy things to be in contact with greatness. Fortunately, Jesus was looking for Zacchaeus because He wanted to tell him that He was going to his house that day.

That was probably one of the greatest moments in Zacchaeus's life! It wasn't just the fact that Jesus was coming to his house, but the fact that He was going to a tax collector's house. I'm sure if you ask your parents they'll tell you they don't like tax collectors either, but back in the day tax collectors were treated like trash. But Jesus changed all that in a moment. And to think that all He did was treat another human being like, well, another human being.

There are going to be kids in your school who aren't as popular as everyone else. In fact, other people may actually laugh at and tease these kids. So here's the cool thing: Why don't you, as a student athlete, try being nice to these "outcast" kids? It takes only one person, and you may start a trend! Jesus took the time to befriend Zacchaeus. If you're a student athlete, or even if you aren't, take the time to make a new friend. Trust me, it's worth it.

Athlete Befriends Bullying Victim

In 2011, former Philadelphia Eagles star DeSean Jackson and some of his buddies appeared on TV to support thirteen-year-old Nadin Khoury. Khoury had recently been beaten up by a group of bullies, and when Jackson heard about it he decided to come to Khoury's side so that no one would ever pick on him again. Jackson even gave Khoury his own jersey!

A friend is one of the nicest things you can have,
and one of the best things you can be.
—Douglas Pagels

What's on Your Plate?

Believe it or not, part of becoming a better athlete is eating properly. Sure, you can get away with eating burgers, fries, and ninety-nine-cent tacos, but that's not what your body needs.

There is a government guide called MyPlate that helps people eat more nutritiously. Each of the different colors represents a food group.

Now, you don't necessarily have to stick to these daily guidelines, but you'll probably be healthier if you move in that direction. Still skeptical? So was Ashpenaz.

According to the Bible, Daniel was a young man without any physical defect and was handsome and smart. That's why the Babylonian king selected him, and other boys like him, to be the king's personal servants.

Daniel 1 says that Daniel told Ashpenaz, his master, that he chose not to defile himself with the royal food and wine. That's a pretty gutsy move. That's like making a sandwich for a homeless person and then having the homeless person tell you that your food isn't good enough.

However, in this case, Daniel had good reason to decline the royal diet. The king's food just wasn't very healthy. Daniel made a wise decision to follow God's eating advice, and Daniel and his friends actually turned out to be better nourished than any of the other young men in the king's court. (In the end, they were ten times smarter than the others, too!) The best part about this story is that it took only ten days to see a difference between Daniel and his friends and those who ate the king's food. All those veggies and that pure water had made an impact!

What you eat is a big part of your lifestyle. Everything you put into your body should have a purpose. Just as with your mind, if garbage goes in, then garbage comes out. So do yourself a favor by eating healthier. I promise that you won't be disappointed by the results!

Leave It on the Floor

No matter what sport you play, there is only one thing your coach wants you to do: leave it on the floor. If you're unfamiliar with the phrase *leave it on the floor*, it means giving your all. You play with all your heart and give your coach 100 percent of your effort. Then, when you feel as if you can't go any further, you dig down and scrape up an extra 10 percent. The point is to exhaust yourself for the cause.

A person cannot truly give their all if they don't care about something. When I was on a team, there were two reasons I played hard every game: I loved what I was doing, and I loved my coaches. I quickly realized that how I played was a direct reflection of how well I was coached. The last thing I wanted to do was give the wrong impression about my coaches' skills!

Many people in the Bible gave their all, but one of the coolest stories I remember is about Elijah. Sometime after the challenge on Mount Carmel, in which Elijah disproved 450 prophets of the false god Baal in front of Israel, Elijah was walking with his successor, Elisha. (Does anyone else always get these two confused?) Anyway, Elijah and Elisha were walking and talking, and as they approached the Jordan, Elijah rolled up his cloak and parted the waters. They continued walking. No big deal. Suddenly a chariot of fire came down from heaven, picked up Elijah, and carried him off to heaven! Words will never do that image justice. Can you imagine seeing a fiery chariot pulled by equally blazing horses? I think God figured that this would be the best way to reward His servant.

During his lifetime Elijah served God with all his heart. Can people say the same thing about you?

Has there ever been a time when you purposely obeyed God

halfheartedly? Such as only obeying your parents sometimes? Or only lying when it was absolutely necessary? All these things add up. Giving your all, whether it's on or off the court, is a must.

Within Christianity, only true Christians love God and believe in His principles. Think about it: Would you follow someone whom you don't like? I know I wouldn't. When you truly love someone, you don't want to disappoint them. You fight to do everything in your power to make sure that never happens. When Jesus finally makes His glorious return, I hope He can look at every one of you reading this and say, "Well done, good and faithful servant"(Matthew 25:21, NIV). Give Him your all, and in return He will give you everything.

Your life is not a rehearsal. Don't leave it without giving it your all.
—Anonymous

Clutter in the Courts

I still love my routine when I'm responsible for opening up a gym. I love the sound of my flip-flops slapping against the hardwood as I walk toward the light switch. I love the distinct buzz of the overhead lamps as they flicker on one by one and the light chases back the shadows inside the gym. I take a deep breath and sigh, "This is home." I am at complete peace here. I can shoot for hours and not get tired, because this is my place of solitude. If I find any trash or empty bottles left behind by previous visitors, I clean the mess up without hesitation, because there's nothing worse than playing in a cluttered gym.

When I see people spilling things in a gym or scuffing the floor with their shoes, it almost makes me sick. I think, *How can you do this to a gym? Don't you know you're ruining it?*

If any of you feel the same way I do, then you probably have some idea of how Jesus felt when He saw people selling things in the temple. Jesus was more than sick—He was outraged. His

Father's house was supposed to be a place for worship and meditation, yet these merchants were showing a lack of respect by treating the temple the same as any other building. That's why Jesus ended up flipping tables and clearing everyone out so that order and reverence could be restored.

In 1 Corinthians 6:19, 20, the Bible tells us that we should treat our bodies like a temple, because that's where God is supposed to live. I hate playing basketball in a run-down gym, because it isn't a pleasant atmosphere. It's probably the same feeling with God. We have to be careful not to clutter our "temples" with outside sources. Those things can include TV, music, and even apps! If you have too many of those things, where can God fit in?

God likes it when we make a special effort to clear a place for Him in our hearts, because that's where He wants to be. In Revelation 3:20, the Bible tells us that God is always waiting to come into our hearts—but He'll enter only if we invite Him in. He won't force His way in. If you haven't already done so, take time to clear out the clutter for God so He can feel right at home.

Because our bodies are the temples of the Holy Spirit, we are to care for them intelligently.
—Seventh-day Adventist fundamental beliefs

The Story of a Scar

I have a total of twenty scars on my body. Each one of them tells a story. They are all battle scars from sports injuries.

I have a scar on the back of my head. It came from when someone fouled me in basketball and I hit my head on the corner of the bleachers. It was painful but not as bad as it sounds. There's also this scar over my eyelid from when someone accidentally poked me in the right eye. I had to walk around with surgical glue on the wound for about a week before I could blink again.

There are multiple scars on my hands and arms from diving

for loose balls and scrapping with other players. There are even some scars on my leg from old soccer battles.

I remember that after every newly obtained scar, my friends and I would gather around and proudly display our scars. We'd boast about who had the best scar and why. Come to think of it, I still do that.

Take a look at your body right now. Do you have any scars? Can you remember where they came from? Along the way I could've put bandages on some of these injuries so that they would heal properly, but I didn't. One reason is that I was a boy and didn't really care. The second reason is that I wanted to remember how I got those injuries. My scars were more than blemishes; they were physical representations of a memory.

After Jesus had risen from the grave, He went to see the disciples. John 20 tells how Thomas doubted that Jesus had indeed risen and wouldn't believe it until he touched the scars for himself. In verses 26, 27, Jesus shows up and gives Thomas permission to do as he desired.

The lesson Jesus was trying to teach there was about faith, but my question is: Why did He keep the scars in His hands? This is the Son of man, who healed other people's hands (Matthew, 12:10–13), so why didn't He heal His own?

Jesus' scars were not simply for Thomas's benefit, but for yours and mine as well. Jesus wants us to remember sin and its consequences. Remember, scars show more than imperfections; they also show that you survived. The scars in Jesus' hands will always tell the story of what sin was and how He conquered it.

The scars of others should teach us caution.

—Jerome

The Secret of the Line

How many of you have ever stood in that "good-game line" after games? Back when I played for a team, it didn't make any sense to me. Why would I want to shake hands with the people I'd just beaten—or lost to? Although I never complained, the thought of saying, "Good game," twenty-plus times really annoyed me. I mean, isn't it a little like lying? Not everybody has a good game. What about the kid who missed too many shots? What about the kid who didn't get to play that much? Did they really have good games?

Probably not, but there's a secret to the line: it's all about respect. That's right, r-e-s-p-e-c-t. (Someone should write a song about it.) The reason you get in that line is to show respect to your opponents. You may not want to do it, but you should for the sake of the game. Confused? Let's look at the Bible for a clearer example.

In 2 Samuel 9, King David meets Mephibosheth for the first time. Mephibosheth was Jonathan's son and King Saul's grandson. David and Jonathan had been the best of friends. Unfortunately, Jonathan never got to properly introduce his son to David before he died. So years later, when David was asking about Saul's relatives, Mephibosheth's name popped up. David immediately requested a meeting with him.

Keep in mind that if Saul hadn't turned away from God, Mephibosheth would've been a prince. He would've been royalty instead of a commoner. On the flip side, David didn't really know this guy. All he knew was that he was the son of his former best friend and a grandson of the man who had tried to kill David. Yikes! I can only imagine what sort of things were running through both of their heads that day.

Anyhow, this is where the respect part comes into play. Instead of hating each other because of their differences, out of respect for each other they put the past behind them and became close friends.

Now, I'm not saying that you've got to be BFFs with the people you play against, but you must always show respect. It's a tough thing to do with all the emotion and adrenaline still floating around, but it's important to do it anyway. Showing respect to your opponent says a lot about your character. Among other things, it shows that you're humble, respectable, and mature.

Now that you know the secret of the line, it's your responsibility to pass it on. And if some opponents choose not to respect you, don't stoop to their level. Pray for them. Not everyone can be as mature as you.

Good coaches teach respect for the opposition, love of competition, the value of trying your best, and how to win and lose graciously.
—Brooks Clark

The Statue

"When the people saw that Moses was so long in coming down from the mountain, they gathered around Aaron and said, 'Come, make us gods who will go before us. As for this fellow Moses who brought us up out of Egypt, we don't know what has happened to him' " (Exodus 32:1, NIV).

As human beings, we are constantly looking for guidance. Some people turn toward God, others to different religions, and the rest look within themselves for spiritual enlightenment. Then there's another religion altogether—sports.

I can't lie—sports are incredible! There are so many great athletes and admirable stories. However, there is a trend that I started noticing a couple of years ago that disturbs me, and that is that organizations started erecting statues of great players. Did you know that there are more than seventy-five statues of sports figures around the world? These statues represent players from real life, such as Tim Tebow, to fictional, such as boxer Rocky Balboa.

I don't mind honoring players, but when players are put on a high pedestal, it gives them a godlike status. I've learned that we should never mistake sports figures' talents for their personal lives.

In order to understand what I mean, just look at what happened with Coach Joe Paterno at Penn State. When reports initially broke about some alleged misconduct, not many people knew the sinister things that were truly happening. In time, our hopes were cast down when we found out that Paterno not only knew about the misconduct but he also tried to cover it up.

The residents surrounding University Park, Pennsylvania, where Penn State is located, loved Paterno, affectionately known as "JoPa" to those close to him. In that small town, everyone listened to Paterno, and, yes, they erected a statue in his honor.

Unfortunately for Paterno, this incident showed that he abused the power the people granted him. As a result, people no longer trusted him, and his statue was dismantled and removed.

When Moses was gone for too long, the children of Israel forgot whom they were serving. They became restless and demanded a new leader, one that was tangible. They began praising the golden calf over the God that had already done so much for them. How do you think that made God feel?

Every now and again, it's easy to get caught up in an athlete's breaking a record, but it's important to remember who created that athlete. Let's remember to honor the Creator and not the created.

I have so many things to work on and so many ways that I fail, but that's what grace is all about. . . . And I constantly wake up every morning, trying to get better, trying to improve, trying to walk closer to God.

–Tim Tebow

The Power of Thoughts

Hard work plus opportunity equals success. For the past couple of years, this has been my motto. It is something that has driven me.

Mottoes such as No Pain, No Gain, Strong to the Finish, and many more have all helped athletes focus their thoughts to complete whatever task they need to finish.

For a time, I was super depressed about not being where I wanted to be in life. But it was in those dark times that I kept telling myself, "Hard work plus opportunity equals success." I repeated that phrase over and over until things such as this book became a reality for me. I truly believe that when you work hard, eventually there will be an opportunity for you to succeed.

Many sports psychologists encourage using mottoes and helpful sayings for positive reinforcement. During high-pressure situations our minds can often sink to negative thoughts that can mentally bring us down. A strong motto doesn't prevent this, but it does help justify the pain we feel in that moment and helps us get through it. It's sort of like a natural painkiller.

The best source of "pain medication," though, is the Bible. It is full of wisdom that can help us through any situation. Many of my favorite bits of inspired wisdom are found in Ecclesiastes and Proverbs. If I ever need advice on anything, those are my go-to books of the Bible.

Elsewhere in the Bible there are ten powerful principles that we as Christians already follow. Any idea what they might be? If you said the Ten Commandments, you're right. Hopefully they have already shaped your life for the better.

Philippians 4:8 tells us to think on things that are pure, noble, and true. By having a motto that embodies these ideals, you'll focus less on the negative and more on the positive.

As an athletic director, each year I have all my sports teams pick a motto for the season. I want them to identify with those words and embody them. It's exciting to see the unique mottoes they come up with. If you haven't done so already, pick a motto that you want to live by. Trust me, you won't regret it.

Finally, brothers and sisters, whatever is true, whatever is noble, whatever is right, whatever is pure, whatever is lovely, whatever is admirable–if anything is excellent or praiseworthy–think about such things.
–Philippians 4:8, NIV

Are You in Good Hands?

A baseball in my hands isn't worth all that much. But a baseball in Justin Verlander's hand is worth about $20 million. A football in my hands isn't worth a whole lot either. However, a football in Tom Brady's hands is worth about $10 million. A basketball in my hands? Well, I like to think I've got some skill in that area, so someone might treat me to an ice-cream cone after a game–if we'd won. A basketball in Kevin Durant's hands, though, is worth $17 million.

These superstar athletes get paid as much as they do because they know what to do when the ball is in their hands. Verlander knows whether to throw the fastball or go for the slider. Brady knows when it's time to step forward through the pocket while managing the clock and his teammates. When a basketball game is on the line, Durant knows whether he should pull up for the jumper or drive to the basket. When the experts have the ball in their hands, more often than not they're going to come through. If you placed me in any of these professional, high-pressure situations, well, I'd fail miserably.

There are countless stories in the Bible that illustrate the difference between when humans take control and when God takes control. The children of Israel probably had the worst time remembering this. After God had arranged for them to leave

Egypt, the Israelites complained about not having an escape route. That's when God used Moses' staff to part the Red Sea. Then they complained about not having good food, so God gave them manna. The list of complaints go on, but probably one of the worst incidents was when they took things into their own hands and built a golden calf to worship. Moses had been on the mountaintop talking with God, and the Israelites grew restless. Instead of waiting patiently, they decided to build their own god in the image of a calf. Big mistake. Among other things, they ended up drinking some very bitter water.

When Moses' time to lead Israel came to an end, he had one last bit of advice for them. In chapter 8 of Deuteronomy, Moses warns the people never to forget God's commands. He reminds them that God will always be there for them no matter how bad the situation might seem. Moses wanted Israel to learn to trust in God because He was and still is the expert at everything. When we invite God to be in charge of our lives, we can know that everything will be all right.

I have held many things in my hands, and I have lost them all;
but whatever I have placed in God's hands, that I still possess.
–Martin Luther

Is It Worth It?

Over the past couple of years I've noticed a growing trend in sports. It seems that athletes are willing to do just about anything to get out of working hard. In the past decade, I've seen an outbreak of steroids in most sports. From Lance Armstrong in cycling to Alex Rodriguez in baseball, a lot of athletes have taken the wide path instead of the straight and narrow one.

Lakers shooting guard Kobe Bryant went to Germany to have surgery on his knee. The procedure is illegal in the United States; that's why Bryant had to go to Germany to get it done. It involves drawing blood from his arm and placing it in his knee so as to regenerate the tissue faster. Weird, right? It gets even weirder.

It was reported just before Super Bowl XLVII that Baltimore Ravens linebacker Ray Lewis took a substance called deer antler spray. Apparently the extract from a deer's antlers can help speed recovery. Hmmm.

The list of those who've tried to gain an advantage through less-than-ethical means goes on for days.

Wouldn't it be great if you could snap your fingers and instantly become a star athlete in any sport? Unfortunately it doesn't work that way. It takes a lot of hard work and dedication to become great in any sport. Right now I can walk into any team practice and tell who the hard workers are.

Did you know that the way you practice ultimately defines your character? Are you the type to follow drill instructions and always give 100 percent, or do you sometimes cheat at the drill just to finish it?

It amazes me to see how many people try to cheat their way to success. Trust me, people, it doesn't pay off. If you're one of the athletes who sees others cheating in practice, don't follow them. Keep working hard on doing your best, and you will be rewarded for your efforts.

Psalm 37:7 says: "Do not fret when people succeed in their ways, when they carry out their wicked schemes" (NIV). God sees all. He knows when people cheat, even when a coach can't see them. It's pretty easy to cheat, but there's a certain reward that comes from doing things the right way and finding the success that it brings. Don't get caught up when others around you don't do the right thing. Always ask yourself, Is it worth it? And you know the answer. (If not, it's the two middle letters of the third word in the previous sentence!)

In Sports We Trust

The Boston Marathon suffered a tragic bombing in 2013. Within a few days one suspect was killed and another was captured. Unfortunately, this wasn't the first time a terrorist plot was launched during a high-profile athletic event.

Terrorist acts took place in both the 1972 and 1996 Olympic Games. In 1972, at the Olympics in Munich, Germany, the Israeli national team was kidnapped. Eventually eleven members of the team were killed. In 1996, at the Atlanta Olympic Games, a bomb killed two people and injured more than one hundred.

That same year in Manchester, England, a cargo van filled with explosives blew up and injured about two hundred people. At the time, England was hosting the European Football Championship.

You get the picture—bad things can happen at sporting events. Following each of these tragedies, the emotional climate was the same. Fear was in the atmosphere, and a sense of uncertainty and worry was in the hearts and minds of everyone affected. It's during such times that people need something to put their trust in. Often, people look beyond the immediate event—including sports venue–related tragedies—and seek out sports as a way to get back to normal. After all, sports can unite everyone, at least momentarily.

At the first sporting events following the Boston bombings, the American national anthem was sung with more pride than usual. This was what connected people in our country, so this was what they put their trust in. As long as the national anthem was sung and there was a competitive sports event happening to distract them, everything would be OK.

For Christians, it's different. Although it's OK that nonbelievers found something to put them at ease and help them return to daily life, it's a little bit like building their trust on sandy ground. Believers, on the other hand, know that when crazy things happen, our trust in God will see us through. After all, He holds the entire world in His hands! He cares for us and is there to comfort us when we feel scared and confused.

Sadly, there will probably be more acts of terror that take place at sporting events across the world. In times like these, we can choose to place our trust in God. He promises never to leave us or forsake us (see Deuternomy 31:6).

Some trust in chariots and some in horses,
but we trust in the name of the LORD *our God.*
They are brought to their knees and fall,
but we rise up and stand firm.
—Psalm 20:7, 8, NIV

Embrace the Struggle

Many of you have probably heard about the exercise program P90X. But have you heard about how dangerous it can be? For those who haven't seen P90X in action, it involves a rapid combination of exercises strung together at a furious pace. There are many people who endorse using P90X because of the wonderful results it gives: toned arms, washboard abs, and bulging muscles. However, I read one article of a firsthand account that wasn't quite as impressive.

Matt Lombardi was a young guy who, after a couple years of inactivity, had tried to start the P90X program from the beginning. The good news is that he completed the first day. The bad news is that he felt really sore. Then the bad went to worse. Lombardi went to the restroom and saw that his urine was the color of root beer. Long story short, he went to the hospital and found out that he had rhabdomyolysis. It's a big word that describes a situation in which the muscles in the body are under too much stress and release toxins into the bloodstream. This in turn causes the kidneys to fail. If the kidneys fail, the body can't purify itself.

While the body is an amazing thing, it does have its limits. Lombardi learned this the hard way. (By the way, he's OK.)

This story illustrates an important lesson. Lombardi couldn't make it through P90X because he'd been inactive for too long. His muscles simply weren't ready to handle that kind of pressure. He needed to get fit, for sure, but he went about it the wrong way. True, a less intense training program still would have been a struggle for him, at least at first. It would've taken longer, but the end result would've been a strong body.

In Romans 5:3, 4, the apostle Paul says: "We also glory in our sufferings, because we know that suffering produces perseverance; perseverance, character; and character, hope" (NIV).

Sometimes to become spiritually fit, you have to let God allow you to struggle over a period of time. Otherwise you might end up unprepared when facing a spiritual battle.

At first the drills I had to do for basketball practice were painful. The only reason I didn't quit was that I knew they would help me in the game. And guess what? All those drills paid off. Now when I coach players to do those same drills, I can smile. I know the players may complain about how hard the drills are, but I know going through them will make them better players. I like to think that's how God looks at us. Whatever tough stuff we're going through, it'll only make us stronger Christians in the end.

I don't know what struggles you're going through, but continue trusting in God. He can make blessings come out of bad things.

Adversity causes some men to break; others to break records.
—William Arthur Ward

Siblings in Sports

I wish I could've played sports with my brother in high school. My brother is about five years older than I am, so this wouldn't have been possible, but it makes a nice daydream. When I watch some of the different professional sports, it's fun to see siblings playing with or against each other.

Arguably two of the most famous siblings in sports, Venus and Serena Williams, have dominated the tennis world since 1997. When they are focused, the duo is almost an unbeatable combination. Together they have thirteen finals appearances in doubles tournaments and have won thirteen titles.

Switching over to Formula 1 racing, Michael Schumacher and his brother, Ralf, are both legends within the sport. Michael, the older brother, is considered one of the greatest racers of all time. He and his brother are the only siblings in the sport to have won races and also finish in first and second places in the same race.

In basketball there is Pau and Marc Gasol. Both are European players who have performed marvelously in the NBA. Pau, the older brother, is smaller than Marc, but Pau has won more championship rings. In the NBA, the Gasol brothers play on opposite teams, but during the world championships, they both play for their national home team, Spain.

Finally, in football we have Peyton and Eli Manning. The older brother, Peyton, was highly scouted in college because he was perceived as the next great football quarterback. The media hype surrounding Peyton quickly drowned out Eli. Peyton rose to the occasion and proved himself as one of the greatest and smartest players in NFL history. But now Eli has also risen to the top of fans' minds as another elite quarterback. They have played against each other only three times.

At the end of the day, that's what it's all about: relationships. All these siblings may be fierce competitors once the game starts, but after it's done, they go back to being siblings. God created families for this very purpose. He wants us to love and build one another up. Although your siblings may get on your nerves sometimes, they are still your siblings. God wants us to treat them with utmost respect.

I greatly admire my older brother. We've shared so many battles in different sports, but no matter how many battles I've won or lost, I still love my brother very much. How is your relationship with your siblings? And if you don't have any siblings, then close friends count as well!

A brother is a friend God gave you; a friend is a brother your heart chose.
–Anonymous

Shout It Out!

Last season I had the pleasure of being involved with a championship varsity basketball team. It was a phenomenal experience. One thing that helped make the season even more memorable was the pregame chant.

Before each game started, the players would encircle the captain. The captain would then look every one of the players in the eye before tilting back his head and yelling, "Whoooooo's got my back?" The players would yell in response, "I've got your back!" The captain would yell again, this time with more emphasis, "Whoooooo's got my back?" And once again the players would reply in unison, "I've got your back!" This back and forth chant would continue, becoming faster and more rhythmic with each round until it reached near-fever pitch. At that point, the players would yell in unison and make an even tighter circle before giving one final shout. Then the game would begin.

After the season was over, I began paying more attention to chants. There are high school varsity chants, college sports chants, and others. Even the US men's national soccer team picked up the chant of "I Believe." (Check it out on YouTube if you haven't heard it.)

The team chant that I find most striking is the one used by the New Zealand national rugby team. It's called haka.

Originally, haka was a traditional ancestral war cry, dance, or challenge from the Maori people of New Zealand. These people would do haka in unison with vigorous movements and rhythmic foot stomping. They believed that if they didn't chant and move in unison, it would bring bad luck before their battle, so everyone had to be united. I don't know if the New Zealand rugby team believes in good and bad luck, but I do know they want to be united once they hit the playing field.

The Bible contains several examples of how being united brought victory. For example, in Joshua 6:6–20, the Israelites marched around the walls of Jericho for seven days. Then, on the seventh day, the priests blew the trumpets, and the people shouted with a great shout. And the walls came down!

Another example is found in Judges 7:20, 21. In this story, Gideon and his three hundred men surrounded the camp of Midian, blew their trumpets, and shouted, "A sword for the LORD and for Gideon" (verse 20, NIV). They went on to defeat the Midianites in battle.

But there is a shout of unity still to come. In Zephaniah 1:16, it mentions that there will be a battle cry on the day of the Lord—that is, when Jesus returns to earth to take His followers home. That really will be something to shout about!

Build for your team a feeling of oneness, of dependence upon one another, and of strength to be derived by unity.
—Vince Lombardi

Too Much Bread and Games

Recently I came across the Latin phrase *panem et circenses*. When translated into English, it means "bread and circuses" or "bread and games." Apparently, this phrase was in reference to the fall of the great Roman Empire. So what does this phrase really mean?

Rome was considered a great city because it played such a significant role in the development of civilizations even after its fall. Among other things, Rome had a great government and military, amazing architecture and engineering, and a fabulous daily life for Roman citizens.

Games were a huge part of Roman citizens' lives. People who attended the games were given free bread. Eventually, though, the Roman Empire fell. One of the many things that contributed to this was the fact that the Roman citizens *stopped doing their civic duty*. They started caring only about the games and free bread. The people of Rome chose to ignore their city and regular responsibilities in favor of attending the games.

With all the new technology we have, sports are now accessible 24-7. It's very easy to get caught up in the wide world of sports. Just think about it: a person can play sports all throughout the school year. Then there are summer sports for you to enjoy during the off-season. You can also watch sports on ESPN, and all the other major networks have their own sports channels. If one TV network isn't enough, you can always choose to watch YouTube, where you can watch highlights of amateur and professional athletes at any hour.

Sports are a great hobby, but they can also be a deadly distraction. We must be careful to live a balanced life. When we begin to reject our duties as Christians and focus only on our hobbies, such as sports, we become unbalanced.

Some of us have been blessed with the gift of athleticism. However, we must use this gift to bring others closer to God and not just for mindless entertainment, or, as they say in Latin, for bread and games.

"My people are destroyed from lack of knowledge.
Because you have rejected knowledge,
I also reject you as my priests;
because you have ignored the law of your God,
I also will ignore your children."
—Hosea 4:6, NIV

The Power of Names

Throughout history, some sports players have earned a nickname. Usually their nickname came from the way that they played.

Michael Jordan's official nickname is "Air." He got this because when he played, he was able to seemingly float on air. Another memorable nickname is The Great One. This was used for Wayne Gretzky because he was considered the greatest hockey player of all time. Legend has it that he was so good that professional hockey players asked for his autograph even though he was too young to be a professional himself!

Walter "Sweetness" Payton was remembered as one of the best running backs of all time. His moves on the field matched his sweet personality off the field. His coach, Mike Ditka, described him as the "greatest football player he had ever seen—but even greater as a human being."*

As I was reading through the New Testament, I started noticing that some of Jesus' disciples had nicknames too! Did you know that James and John were nicknamed the "Sons of Thunder"? The Bible doesn't say exactly why, but if you pay attention to the brothers' attitudes, you'll see that they could be very hot-tempered and unforgiving.

Though He does not exactly have nicknames, Jesus was called several different things. John the Baptist called Him the Lamb of God. Jesus referred to Himself as the Son of man. His disciples called Him Master. In different parts of the Bible, He's called Savior, Redeemer, Emmanuel, and so on. Each of these names has its own special meaning, and they all represent different characteristics of Jesus.

While at a basketball tournament in high school, a guy named Mike gave me the nickname One Man Show. When I asked him

---

* Michael Lichtenstein, "Never Die Easy: The Autobiography of Walter Payton," *The New York Times*, October 15, 2000, https://archive.nytimes.com/www.nytimes.com/books/00/10/15/bib/001015.rv080804.html.

why, he told me that I did "everything" out there on the court. My nickname described how I strived to play the game.

Having a nickname helps a person focus. Having my nickname gave me purpose on the court because I realized that I needed to live up to it. If I felt this way, imagine how Jesus feels with all of His designations? Master. Savior. Redeemer. He lives up to those three names and more.

Do you have a nickname? If so, does it make you play or live differently? If Jesus were to give you a nickname, what would it be? Think about your characteristics and how you treat others. Try to think of a good nickname for yourself and live up to it. You'll be surprised just how much a nickname can help determine how you live.

Words have meaning and names have power.
–Anonymous

What Are You Listening To?

Beats headphones had a meteoric rise in popularity. Athletes such as Serena Williams, Colin Kaepernick, Matt Kemp, and many others are all huge supporters and are often seen wearing the brand. Part of the reason these headphones are so popular is that they not only look cool but also claim to be the best at canceling out external noises. In reality, they are probably not the best at canceling noise. But noise canceling is an important feature, because usually nothing should interrupt what you hear.

Awhile back, Beats had a series of commercials that featured athletes blocking out everything else and listening to only what was coming through their headphones. My favorite commercial featured NBA player Kevin Garnett. (I once met him, but that's another story.) Anyway, the commercial started off with Garnett sitting on a team bus traveling to a game. The bus arrives at the other team's stadium, and there are fans yelling and screaming at Garnett in a effort to throw him off his game. The rowdy fans then begin throwing things at the team bus! But Garnett doesn't react; he simply puts on his Beats headphones, and all of a sudden it's pure silence. The fans' angry words are now canceled out. Garnett then smiles as his favorite song begins to play. The crowd continues to yell, but he can't hear them, because he has his headphones on. As the commercial fades, the words "Hear What You Want" appear on the screen. I love this commercial because it emphasizes the importance of blocking out all external noises in order to concentrate on things that will help us achieve internal success.

In 1 Kings 19, we find a distressed Elijah in hostile territory. God told Elijah to wait for Him on top of a mountain. Elijah obeyed and waited. First there was a huge wind that ripped through the mountain, but that wasn't God. Next there was a big earthquake, but that wasn't God either. Along came a fire, but again it wasn't God. After the fire came a gentle whisper. It was God! And that's when Elijah finally heard from his heavenly Father.

In life, there will be noises that distract you. Your success will be determined by your ability to mute the external noise and listen to the still, small Voice. This is when you have the best opportunity to hear God speak. Headphones or no headphones, it's up to you to hear what you need to hear. What are you listening to?

This section was inspired by and dedicated to Ryan Johnson, who reminded me of the importance of blocking out the noise and being comfortable with silence.

The silence of the soul makes more distinct the voice of God.
—Ellen White

Crowns

The Isthmian Games started back around 582 B.C. These games were very similar to the Olympics. At the Isthmian Games, the athletes competed in wrestling, boxing, and chariot races. Like the Olympics, the Isthmian Games came around only every couple of years, so the athletes had to train constantly. They probably trained every day, and it would have been intense because the athletes knew that, even after months of hard training, they had only one shot to win against the other athletes who were competing.

So what was the prize for winning at the Isthmian Games, you might ask? It was a wreath made from celery. Yes, celery—the vegetable. Later the wreath would be made from pine leaves, but all that practicing still seems like quite a lot of work for a vegetable crown. Can you imagine training hard for months, only to have such a prize as that? It doesn't seem as if it would be worth it, does it?

This is exactly what Paul was talking about in 1 Corinthians 9:24–27. Many people like to use verse 24 to compare sports to Christianity. Verse 24 talks about running the race to get the prize. While this is a great analogy, without the next verses the message loses some power. Verses 25–27 focus on how everyone who competes in these games goes into strict training—but only to get a crown (prize) that will not last. I've personally never worn a crown made from celery or pine leaves, but I imagine that I wouldn't want to keep something such as that for more than a week. So Paul is stating that if we train so hard for things that won't last, then we should train even harder for something that will.

Our society places a lot of emphasis on winning, so it's not hard to imagine why we're so obsessed with it. We play hard to win this game or that tournament. We spend our nights and weekends practicing. We watch YouTube clips to see what the latest moves are. Some of us will go as far as losing sleep, stopping studying our schoolwork, and even abandoning our time with God.

As much fun as it is to play sports, we must always remember that we're part of a much bigger competition—the prize for which is much greater than we can imagine. However, just as in any other competition, this will not be an easy victory. The enemy is constantly trying to make us fail. We have to practice hard every day, understanding that it takes time, effort, and a lot of help from our heavenly Father to succeed. Just think: if a crown of thorns marked Jesus' victory, then He definitely has a better crown for us.

We all have dreams. In order to make dreams come into reality, it takes an awful lot of determination, dedication, self-discipline, and effort.
—Jesse Owens

Embracing Conflict

One of my favorite parts of watching sports is the behind-the-scenes moments. With today's technology the cameras are always recording. Good or bad, everything an athlete or team does is under a microscope.

As I was watching a very intense game, there was a time-out called. During the break, two players were having what looked like an argument. Both players were dramatically moving their hands to show what they meant. It was obvious that the players didn't agree about something. It became such a spectacle that all the cameras were now watching them. One of the announcers for the game made a general statement about how the players were mad at each other and that this could be a bad sign for the team. Then one of the other announcers said something that stuck with me. He said, "I don't mind this sort of conflict. These are two competitors trying to figure out the best way to win. This is good conflict."

The announcer went on to explain that as a former player himself he had been through many moments like this before. These moments were healthy because it allowed the players to grow as a team. Good conflict was strange for me to hear, because I was always taught that conflict was bad. If there was conflict, then something wasn't right.

That's when the light bulb clicked on for me. The beauty of seeing conflict among players, even the great ones, is that no team is perfect. Conflict is inevitable: you can't avoid it; it's going to happen. At its worst, you'll see tempers flare as players or coaches throw or kick things in a display of their rage. At its best, you'll see a problem being solved in real time as players or coaches discuss how best to tackle an issue. It's the way conflict is managed that determines how successful a team can be.

In the Bible, James asks, "What is the source of quarrels and conflicts among you?" (James 4:1, NASB). He then goes on to point out that the issue is usually selfishness, also known as pride. By speaking to one another in love (see 1 Corinthians 13), we'll be less prideful when trying to solve conflicts with our teammates. This helps us warm up for tackling the issue; sort of like stretching before a game. Finally, in Matthew, Jesus told us to handle our problems as quickly as possible (Matthew 5:23–25), do it face-to-face (Matthew 18:15), and to also ask for help if we need it (Matthew 18:16, 17).

The great thing is that this doesn't apply just to sports. You can use these techniques anywhere. Good conflict allows us to grow closer to those around us, so don't avoid it; embrace it.

Peace is not absence of conflict; it is the ability to handle conflict by peaceful means.
—Ronald Reagan